MW01244159

'At a Glance' Religious & Spiritual Competency for Psychotherapists

By: Janine d'Haven MA, MDiv.

Bloomington, IN

authorHOUSE™

Milton Keynes, UK

AuthorHouse™
1663 Liberty Drive, Suite 200
Bloomington, IN 47403
www.authorhouse.com
Phone: 1-800-839-8640

AuthorHouse™ UK Ltd.
500 Avebury Boulevard
Central Milton Keynes, MK9 2BE
www.authorhouse.co.uk
Phone: 08001974150

This book is a work of non-fiction. Unless otherwise noted, the author and the publisher make no explicit guarantees as to the accuracy of the information contained in this book and in some cases, names of people and places have been altered to protect their privacy.

© 2006 Janine d'Haven MA, MDiv.. All rights reserved.

No part of this book may be reproduced, stored in a retrieval system, or transmitted by any means without the written permission of the author.

First published by AuthorHouse 6/7/2006

ISBN: 1-4259-0684-2 (sc)

Printed in the United States of America
Bloomington, Indiana

This book is printed on acid-free paper.

© Janine d'Haven, MA. MDiv, IFCM May 2003

Forward

A new client sat across from me telling me her story and reasons for wanting therapy. As she explained her feelings of hopelessness her emotional state began to deteriorate. When I asked her how long she had these feelings she said it began long ago when she realized she was doomed to an afterlife of torment so terrible she couldn't bear thinking about it. She began to cry uncontrollably, almost hyperventilating. She said she couldn't bear this life, and was scared of taking her own life because she would find no relief in death.

When she began to calm, I gently probed into her belief of the afterlife. She explained that her Mormon upbringing taught that there are three levels of afterlife, and that she was certain she would be sent to the worst level to live her human suffering and misery for all eternity. I thought to myself, "I wish I had gotten to the point in my thesis that explained the Mormon belief of the afterlife. It sure would come in handy right now."

It is my opinion that beliefs and religious teachings are transmitted through the family and begin early in the lives of many people. A result is an interweaving of religious beliefs, ethnic and cultural family dynamics, and personal development to form worldviews. I believe this also is true for those who may not participate in formal or organized religion but have strong spiritual beliefs that may have been passed down from generation to generation. To understand the individual it is imperative to understand their earlier and present environment.

Many people's lives are immersed in religious and spiritual beliefs. Polling data from the 2001 *ARIS* study indicates that: 81% of American adults identify themselves with a specific religion. The title of Diane Eck's book makes an accurate and eye opening statement: "A New Religious America: How a 'Christian Country' has become the world's most religiously diverse nation" (Eck, 2001).

So I welcome you to "At a Glance" manual for religious and spiritual competency for psychotherapists and all mental health practioners. I began writing this manual for my own personal use when I was half way through my Master's degree in Counseling and Psychology. Prior to my MA studies I had attended an Interfaith Seminary Program for four years where I developed a broad and strong understanding of the vast and diverse landscape of religion and spiritual beliefs. Now faced with the newly revealed landscape of the human mind and psyche, I wanted to have a deeper understanding of the implications religious and spiritual teachings have on an individual's psychology.

Since religious/spiritual teachings are interwoven into the psyche, understanding belief systems improves the ability to communicate with clients.

It didn't make sense to rack my brain trying to remember the important points of various religious and spiritual traditions. And reaching for one of the numerous books on religious and spiritual traditions wasn't feasible. Therefore this manual is designed as a quick, at a glance, reference and reminder of what various traditions believe and teach.

This manual is not designed to teach religion. Nor is it a substitute for developing strong multicultural competence. It only proposes a guide to working with spiritual and religiously diverse clients. Its function is to give the therapist a brief "heads up" regarding a clients religious teachings, views, specific issues to be aware of, and technique suggestions to

assist therapists when working with clients from various traditions.

The included information can also be used as a compass for religious/spiritual beliefs that are not represented. It can hopefully steer the reader in the right direction of inquiry. My hope is that you the reader will reflect carefully and critically when reading and then, through incorporation, develop a personal framework that is congruent with your values, professional commitments and ethics, and areas and theories of practice.

Before we start I would like to make two important definition distinctions:

The term spiritual refers to a consciousness not of the body, a transcendent relationship with a Higher Existence whether called the Divine, God, Great Spirit, etc. This relationship includes guidance, peace, love, awe, reverence, and inspiration.

The term religious refers to a particular system of worship, ritual, practice of faith, and rules of conduct.

Religious expressions are more denominational, external, behavioral, cognitive, ritualistic, and public, while spiritual experiences tend to be universal, inclusive, internal, affective, private (Richards & Bergin, 1999). What's also important to know is that it is possible to be spiritual and not religious or vice versa, though some people are both spiritual and religious.

Main Sources of Information for this Manual
Handbook of Psychotherapy and Religious Diversity, P. Scott Richards
and Allen E. Bergin, 2000.Eds.
The Handy Religious Answer Book by John Renard, 2002
Religions of America by Leo Rosten, 1975
A Brief Guide to Beliefs, Ideas, Theologies, Mysteries, and
Movements by Linda Edwards
Integrating Spirituality into Multicultural Counseling by Mary
Fukuyama and Todd Sevig
Assessing Culturally Diverse Clients by Freddy Paniagua
Counseling the Culturally Diverse 4th Edition by Derald Wing
Sue and David Sue
Complete Bibliography can be found at the back of the manual

Included in this Manual

Introduction
Spiritual Assessment

**Included in each of the following Religious or Spiritual Traditions
you will find the following categories:**
- Beliefs
- Practices
- View of a Deity
- View of Afterlife – Death & Dying
- Moral views on issues such as sex, marriage and divorce, birth control and abortion, suicide/euthanasia, and the use of medicine, alcohol and illicit drugs.
- Views of mental health professionals and therapy
- Treatment Recommendations
- Assessment tools
- Common clinical issues
- Intervention strategies
- Estimated population of adherents

Table of Contents

Chapter One

The religious landscape of North America is vast and diverse. Members of all the major religions such as Christianity, Judaism, and Islam, and many other religions such as Buddhism, Hinduism, and those who practice Latin Spirituality have made their homes here. It is not uncommon for one to interact with several individuals from different cultural backgrounds and worldviews on a daily basis making religious diversity a cultural fact. America has always been a cultural and religiously diverse nation and is currently the "most profusely religious nation on earth" (Eck, 2001).

As immigration, world consciousness, individualism, and knowledge availability through the media and the Internet increases, the landscape is quickly changing and becoming more intricate in what it has to offer the spiritual and/or religious seeker. Each spiritual and religious tradition brings with it a rich tapestry of customs, beliefs, worldviews, doctrines, myths, rituals, music, places of worship, clothing, sacred writings, spiritual practices, and healing traditions. As the population of the United States increases in the diversity of religious, social, and cultural backgrounds, competence in multicultural counseling has never been greater.

An important aspect in achieving cultural sensitivity and competence is the understanding of the spiritual and/or religious belief systems and worldviews within various cultures. "An

1

awareness of client's worldviews can guide us toward developing the skills needed for effectiveness in cross-cultural counseling and psychotherapy" (Ibrahim, 1985, p. 626). Worldviews are defined as being composed of attitudes, values, opinions, concepts and philosophies of life construed through the lenses of peoples' cultural upbringing. Worldview inherently involves a person's religious and spiritual beliefs. Acknowledging the relationship that religion and spirituality has, as part of the culture of most people, is a way to honor and show respect for a client's beliefs across cultural and religious differences.

Many people who immigrate to the U.S. formally lived in cultures that express their spiritual and religious views as a matter of daily life. This also applies to many people born in the U.S. who live and have been raised in families that have similarly strong belief systems. For many these views are an integral part of their life development and impact all psychological developmental levels (Worthington, 1989). Therefore, the life development of many people cannot be adequately understood without an appreciation of the spiritual/religious dimension. Throughout life development a specific way of expressing oneself develops which includes their views as spiritual or religious language.

It is potentially difficult for mental health practitioners to listen to and interpret material clients bring to treatment when that material involves spiritual/religious beliefs or religious language. One aspect of religious language is when a client reports psychological experiences in religious language. Common religious language examples include: "God is punishing me for [...]," "Why did He let this happen?" "Spirits are making my mind crazy." This last example is especially ripe with potential misunderstanding. It is of vital importance for clients and their therapists to have a mutual understanding, and one way is mutual language. If the 'language' the client understands best is religious then I must be prepared to speak with them in ways and words they understand.

I gained first hand knowledge of the value of religious competence and God language while volunteering at a refugee clinic as a Minister/Therapist. A devout, Roman Catholic, Hispanic woman was referred to me for counseling. She had previously been referred to a Psychiatrist to discuss stressful life situations that were exacerbating her illnesses. She reported to me that she went to one appointment, but because 'God was her therapist' and the Psychiatrist didn't understand this religious conviction, she refused to return for further appointments. When I explained I was a Minister as well as a Therapist, we were able to move beyond her initial resistance and initiate a therapeutic relationship. I utilized her "God language," the language that provided the most comfort, and conducted several therapy sessions with positive outcomes measured by her decreased stress and enhanced health and well-being.

As a mental health practitioner I find it imperative to be able to understand the spiritual/religious orientations of my clients as a means of understanding their lives. I agree with David Wulf when he stated, "No other human preoccupation challenges psychologists as profoundly as religion. Whether or not they profess to be religious themselves – and many do not – psychologists must take religion into account if they are to understand and help their fellow human beings" (Wulf, 1991, p. 10).

Because many clients rely on spiritual and religious beliefs and traditions that are embedded in their cultural background to cope with problems, it is very important that therapists understand how these beliefs are linked to the way people react to problems they encounter in their lives. I believe as therapists in an ever-changing multicultural landscape, it is not only our professional but also our ethical responsibility to expand our understanding of religious diversity leading to increased credibility and influence. For clients, it could increase the likelihood that they will receive the mental health services they need from someone who understands their perspective and who does not automatically interpret their religious/spiritual beliefs in pathological terms (Bergin & Richards, 1999, p. 11).

An understanding of religious, cultural and ethnic beliefs could open doors to clients we might not have been able to assist. The following statistics illuminate the necessity of religious competence:

- 60% of APA psychologists report clients often express their personal experiences in religious language (Bergin & Richards, 1999).
- 72% of psychologists indicate that they had addressed religious or spiritual issues in treatment (Lannert, 1991).
- 1 in 6 clients present with issues which directly involve religion or spirituality (Shafranske & Maloney, 1990).
- 39% of the U.S. population are practicing Roman Catholics (Bedell, 1997).

The client's perspective on religion or spirituality is a critical aspect of most cultures and one that is a focal point for a significant number of clients who seek psychological treatment (Shafranske, 1996, p. 564). Therefore, emphasis has been placed on therapists having a professional and ethical responsibility to expand their understanding of religious diversity. This leads to increased credibility and positive influence in order to help intervene on mental illness. For many therapists, intensive multicultural studies during and after licensure is required to maintain their license thus the importance of expanding this aspect is recognized as being of vital import.

Since it is the ethical responsibility for all mental health practitioners to stay current with new developments in the field and develop an understanding of the beliefs and values of culturally diverse clients, we are lead to the importance of developing competency in the spiritual and religious beliefs of clients (Watts, 2001). From my review of recent professional literature I can safely say that the majority of experts agree that, though incorporating spirituality and religion with the field of psychology will be a long and arduous road to walk, it is a necessary one since many clients can be successfully treated *only* if their spiritual issues are addressed sensitively and capably (Shafranske, 1996).

Many in the field of mental health might object to the concept to become more religiously and spiritually informed and sensitive, and might also disagree with the premise that therapists should tune into the healing potential of the worlds religious and spiritual traditions. Objections may be raised on several grounds including the psychological, physical and emotional harm that some of these same religious and spiritual we see as having caused. These objections are absolutely valid. Many harmful acts have occurred in the name of religious and spiritual conviction and so called "truth." But the purpose of increasing religious and spiritual diversity sensitivity is not to endorse any particular belief but to work with them in a manner that contributes to the clients healing. All religious groups have a basic desire to be understood. With the increase in spiritual and religious diversity many therapists don't have no choice but to increase their competence in this area. It is important to remember that literacy or competence in an area does not mean endorsing a particular view.

Spiritual and religious questioning in therapy is not new as religious and spiritual views were excluded from psychotherapy for nearly a century. This omission is coming to an end with the incorporation of these views, perspectives, and interventions into psychological theory, research and practice. This new collaboration of religious and spiritual understanding about values could bring clarity to the therapeutic relationship that wasn't available previously.

What *is* new is the need for fuller recognition by therapists of the importance in incorporating this dimension into their therapeutic relationships. Historically these two areas were split off from one another when psychology became a science. The new paradigm is the re-incorporation of the spiritual dimension. Worthington (1989) cited five reasons for therapists to understand religious faith:

1. A high percentage of Americans consider themselves to be religious.

2. People in emotional crisis often spontaneously consider spiritual and religious matters during periods of intense emotional and psychosocial disorganization.
3. Many clients might have religious issues but feel reluctant to bring them up in therapy.
4. Therapists, by nature and by professional association, generally are more secular than their clients making it difficult to work to maximum benefit with the more religious clients.
5. The lack of religious knowledge on the part of therapists can and does result in their missing important aspects of their client's belief system.

It is interesting that psychotherapy and psychology distanced itself from religious and spiritual views since these same views influence the therapist. The therapist's worldviews influence how they conduct therapy including which theoretical orientations they favor, treatment goals, assessment methods, intervention techniques, and evaluations of therapy outcome. Since the therapist is influenced, then the client must also be influenced.

Green (1982) recommends that professional helpers be aware of their own cultural limitations, be open to cultural differences, and be flexible. It is important for the therapist to inquire and learn about themselves through self-reflection and soul searching. There are many tools available for therapists to identify and/or clarify their biases, beliefs, values, and worldviews. Two resources are the books *Integrating spirituality into multicultural counseling* by Fukuyama and Sevig, and *A spiritual strategy of counseling and psychotherapy* by Richards and Bergin.

One of the first steps to building a more constructive relationship with the members of diverse religious communities is for therapists to "seek training in and a greater appreciation for the religious and spiritual diversity that exists" in the United States (Bergin & Richards, 1999, p. 10). There are many ways therapists can increase their knowledge of religious diversity. I chose to enroll in an Interfaith Seminary program. I studied the world's religions and spiritual belief systems from their historical inception to their contemporary mode of expression, beliefs, values, morals, and rituals. This experience provided me with deep personal spiritual and religious insight. It also provided me foundational information and understanding of the many cultural orientations that make up the diverse spiritual practices and religious beliefs in the North America and the greater global community. Other ways include attending courses in comparative religions, studying the leaders in the field of including spirituality and religious diversity in therapy, speaking with religious leaders in the community and attending rituals, ceremonies, and worship services.

A simple way to begin to expand spiritual and religious awareness is by using this manual. I researched the information regarding counseling and religious/spiritual beliefs through sacred texts, lectures by members of various religious groups, historical information, and a variety of books featuring religious diversity, multicultural counseling and spirituality, personal experience, and contemporary literature on religious diversity in the counseling profession. Though I have specific training in religious/ spiritual issues I recognize that I can only have a partial recall of the vast body of religious and psychotherapeutic material. I realized that if I had a prompter, with key core material previously learned, I could readily access the information I needed during counseling sessions. Therefore, this "At a Glance" manual provides these various prompters.

In conclusion, combining cultural and religious/spiritual beliefs with contemporary Western therapeutic modalities is the most effective way to assist the greatest number of clients (Watts, 2001). Evolvement of multicultural theories is important to the evolution of a counseling practice. Shaping a practice is to craft the practice. I believe that all human contact is multicultural, as we are all individuals, even if we are of similar cultural, spiritual and/or religious up-bringing. As a therapist the challenge is to conduct a practice which honors us all as individuals similar or diverse cultures.

Chapter Two

The Importance of a Religious-Spiritual Client Intake

When first meeting a new patient a Global Assessment or Psychosocial Assessment provides valuable information. Within the Global Assessment a brief Spiritual Assessment can help determine issues related to religious/spiritual beliefs and/or provide insight into cultural issues, while gaining knowledge about the patients world view.

Richards and Bergin (1997) site five reasons to conduct a Religious-Spiritual Assessment: 1. It can help therapists better understand their clients' worldviews, increasing the capacity for increased understanding, 2. It can help determine whether clients' religious-spiritual orientation is healthy or unhealthy and what impact its is having on their present problems, 3. It can help determine whether the clients' religious-spiritual beleifs and/or community could be used as a resource to help them better cope, heal, and grow, 4. It can help determine which spiritual interventions could be used in therapy, 5. Can help determine whether clients' have unresolved religious-spiritual issues, doubts, concerns, or needs that should be addressed in therapy.

Religious-Spiritual Client Intake

Assessment Questions

1. Do you have a religious or spiritual belief?
    If yes, please explain. If no, please explain why not.

    If you've answered "No" please answer questions #2 - #10.
    If you've answered "No" and it is because of a lack of exposure to religion or spirituality in your life, would you like to learn about the spiritual aspects of your life?

2. What do you believe is the purpose of your life?
3. What gives your life meaning?
4. What is most important to you in life?
5. What morals, ethics, or values, if any, guide your life?
6. Do you feel that your behavior and lifestyle are consistent with your values?
7. What are your goals and dreams?
8. Are religious or spiritual issues important in your life?
9. Do you wish to discuss them in counseling, when relevant?
10. Do you believe in a Divine, Supreme Being, or God?
    What do you call this Being?
    Please explain your perception of this Being.
11. Do you believe you can experience spiritual guidance?
    Have you experienced this kind of guidance?
    If yes, please explain.
12. What is your current religious affiliation if any?
13. Are you actively involved in this tradition?
14. What was your religious/spiritual affiliation as a child?

15. Was your childhood experience positive, negative or both?
    Please explain.
16. Do you believe your spiritual beliefs and lifestyle are contributing to your current problems in any way?

If yes, please explain.

17. Are you aware of any religious or spiritual resources available to you that could help you overcome your issues or assist us in therapy?

18. Would you like your counselor to consult with your religious leader if it appears it could help you?

19. Are you willing to try religious or spiritual suggestions from your counselor if it appears they could help you?

Adapted in part from three assessments in A Spiritual Strategy for Counseling and Psychotherapy by Richards and Bergin, 1999, p. 187- 195, as well as, professional experience as a spiritual counselor.

Chapter Three - Abrahamic Traditions

Catholicism has two main denominations Roman Catholic and Eastern Orthodox.

In 100 CE the term "catholic" was used to describe the undivided Christian church. "Catholic" means "geographically universal," (Oxford American Dictionary, 1980) and "broadminded as in beliefs and views" (Magida, 1996).

Two subsequent schisms occurred. The first occurred in 1054 between the eastern and western branches of the church and the term "catholic" became synonymous with the western branch which is under the guidance of the Vatican based in Rome. The Pope is the religious head of the Roman Catholic Church. Roman Catholicism teaches that revelations are summed up in the life and teachings of Jesus Christ who commanded his apostles to teach the Good News, the Gospel.

In the 1500's the second occurred when the Anglo-Catholic – Anglicanism separated from Rome over the Divine Right's of Kings in the 1500's.

The Orthodox Church grew out of the division between eastern and western branches. Eastern Orthodox, sometimes referred to as Greek Orthodox (historically correct name) refers to the early Christians whose members spoke and used Greek thought to find appropriate expressions of their orthodox beliefs. "Orthodox" means true belief. Eastern/Greek Orthodox is catholic (universal) because the whole world is considered its province and because it is universal in time and place (Rosten, 1975) They do not recognize the Pope as final authority and are self-governing.

The differences between these Catholic traditions are in administration of doctrine and practice. Roman Catholics consider the Pope infallible while Eastern Orthodox considers the church infallible.

Roman Catholic

Beliefs
Belief in a God, a Supreme Being who created the universe, the earth, and humans. God is eternal, omnipotent, and all knowing. Catholicism teaches that original sin – Adam and Eve's expulsion from the Garden of Eden for disobeying God – alienated humanity from God. But man and woman have a chance of redemption through the sacraments, the church teachings, and the grace (divine life) of God. Individuals can prove they are just and deserving of life eternal in Heaven.

View of Deity
God loves and assists humans. Trinitarian belief in the unity of God who is understood as God the Father, God (Jesus Christ) the Son, and God the Holy Spirit.
The Catholic faith has belief in the Word of God made flesh in Jesus Christ thus bringing the invisible God into material form.
A special place is accorded to Mary, the mother of Jesus, who was born pure, without original sin. Mary conceived Jesus through Immaculate Conception (Virgin birth), has perpetual virginity, and was assumed body and soul into heaven as was Jesus.

View of the Devil
Catholics believe that Satan (the leader of fallen angels) and his followers are pure spirits of high intelligence used to perpetrate temptation, torment, destruction, and evil.

Spiritual practices and Healing Traditions
This is a Sacramental faith, meaning God is encountered in the seven sacraments of the church. The term Sacrament means Sacred Practice. They are similar to rites of passage occurring at various times throughout life. Participants enter into the divine truths each present. The Sacraments: baptism, confirmation, Eucharist, penance (confession), anointing of the sick, holy orders, matrimony, last rites.

Healing is asked for through prayer, devotional offerings, anointing with oil, and laying on of hands, to name a few.

View of Afterlife

The final goal for Roman Catholics is to enter Heaven. To do this one needs to be forgiven of their sins *and* holy prior to death. If not, the soul resides in purgatory where a final cleansing of sins can occur thus acquiring holiness. For those who die without cleansing their sins their souls are condemned to hell, eternal punishment and suffering (Catechism of Catholic Church, 1994).

Abortion and Birth Control

Abortion and artificial birth control are considered wrong and sinful.

Sexuality

Premarital, homosexual, extramarital sexual behavior is considered sinful. Homosexuality is believed to be a psychological disorder needing treatment.

Marriage and Divorce

Marriage is a holy union and a contract "till death do us part". Civil marriage and divorce doesn't affect the sacramental status of marriage and is not recognized. Separation from "bed and board" (Rosten, 1975) permitted due to abuse. Annulments are occasionally granted. Catholics may not remarry during the lifetime of the ex-spouse.

Alcohol, Illicit Drugs, Gambling

Though alcohol is not considered evil in itself, it may become sinful through excess and abuse. Temperance is encouraged in the use of alcohol and tobacco. Using illicit drugs is considered a grave offense. Gambling is considered harmless unless: the subject of the bet is sinful, one party is ignorant of the terms, cheating or fraud, the money betted should be used for the care of oneself or family, the gambling game is forbidden by law. (Rosten, 1975)

Medicine
Open to the use of medications (except contraception).

Suicide and Direct Euthanasia
These are considered morally unacceptable. The discontinuation of extreme medical treatments may be considered when circumstantially legitimate (passive euthanasia).

View of Therapy
In general therapy is accepted though a variety of opinions can be found. Conservative Roman Catholics may prefer a therapist whose faith perspective is similar to their own.

Religious-clinical issues
Common issues include: authority conflicts, sexuality, inter-religious marriage, divorce, abortion, suicide, artificial insemination, birth control, women's subjugation, genetic engineering, euthanasia, and loss of faith.

Assessment Recommendations
Inquire about past and present religious experiences and affiliations, including religious training, sacraments received, salience of church teaching and authority, use of religious resources, God image, and normative status of religious beliefs and behaviors. Holding beliefs or performing rituals outside of the normative religious experience might suggest a psychological disorder. For example clients who perpetrate injurious behaviors upon themselves (i.e. flagellation, extreme fasting) is suggestive of psychopathology.

Treatment Recommendations
Any psychological intervention would be alright to use. Be aware of the strongly emphasized teachings and beliefs about the meaning of suffering and/or martyrdom, guilt, death, resurrection, confession, and reconciliation. Assess and work through internalized God representations. Look for incongruity between belief and experience. Be sensitive to countertransference issues.

Integrate religious resources and interventions when appropriate. Consult with clergy.

Points about the Clergy
Clergy and Religious often seek professional consultation to strengthen their skills in pastoral counseling and psychological intervention, as well as, to obtain treatment (Richards & Bergins, 2000). The reasons for treatment may be similar to those of the general population and/or could be specific to their vocation. Vocational concerns may arise around issues of celibacy, obedience, intimacy, sexual discrimination and/or segregation. Caution: It is important to remain focused on mental health issues since religious/spiritual counseling to a clergy will probably be beyond the sphere of competence for most clinicians. Women have no clerical function and may not be ordained. They may perform auxiliary tasks for the church.

Self Identified Roman Catholics
2000
63,683,030 Members
(American Religious Identification Survey, 2000)

Eastern Orthodox

Beliefs
They believe the integrity of the teachings of Jesus and the Apostles are preserved unprofaned by the Church. The Bible is the written revelation of God's truths. The church's tradition is under the guidance of the Holy Spirit.

View of Deity
Trinitarian belief in God the Father, God (Jesus Christ) the Son, and the Holy Spirit.
God himself is revealed in Jesus Christ though God is ultimately unknowable, the Ultimate Mystery.

Spiritual practices and Healing Traditions
Center of Orthodox worship is the Divine Liturgy (Mass). Daily prayer morning, afternoon, and evening. Sacramental faith means God is encountered in the seven sacraments of the church. The term Sacrament means Sacred Practice. Participants enter into the divine truths each present. The Sacraments: Liturgy, baptism, chrismation (confirmation), Eucharist, confession, anointing of the sick, holy orders, matrimony, last rites.
Healing is asked for through prayer, devotional offerings, and fasting, to name a few.

View of Afterlife
The final goal for Eastern Orthodox is to enter Heaven. To do this one needs to be forgiven of their sins *and* holy prior to death. If this has not been accomplished the soul resides in intermediate state where the soul glimpses the existence to come, then moves on to it's eternal punishment or bliss.

Abortion and Birth Control
Abortion is forbidden. Contraception is officially condemned, but the choice of use is between spouses.

Sexuality
Premarital, homosexual, and extramarital sex are considered sinful and strictly opposed.

Marriage and Divorce
Marriage is sacred. Divorce is granted when all attempts at reconciliation have failed, and for specific reasons such as adultery, immoral acts, abuse or treacherous actions, abandonment, heresy, and incurable insanity. Remarriage of the innocent party is permitted though not more than three marriages in allowed (Rosten, 1975)

Alcohol, Illicit Drugs
Moderate use of alcohol is acceptable. Drunkenness and use of illegal drugs are condemned.

Medicine
Open to use of medications.

Suicide and Euthanasia
Both are considered morally wrong. Withdrawing life support when appropriate is acceptable.

View of Therapy
Orthodox immigrants will probably be unfamiliar with therapy and are unlikely to seek it or to self disclose. Second and third generation Orthodox and converts may be more open to therapy. It is taught that the Church is the spiritual hospital for the sinner who seeks spiritual health (Richards & Bergin, 2000) Repentance or metanoia is the way to keep sin from becoming a permanent state of being. Repentance is both an internal and external process.

Religious-clinical issues
Be aware of language, cultural assimilation and barriers. Other issues include sexuality, abortion, divorce, humility and obedience.

Assessment Recommendations

Assess the level of client's involvement in the Orthodox faith. Inquire about past and present religious experiences and affiliations, including religious training, sacraments received, salience of church teaching and authority, use of religious resources, God image, and normative status of religious beliefs and behaviors. Holding beliefs or performing rituals outside of the normative religious experience might suggest a psychological disorder.

Treatment Recommendations

Any psychological intervention would be all right to use with the majority of Orthodox persons. It is important to avoid interventions that would influence religious views (Richards & Bergin, 2000). Most Orthodox will not respond well to spiritual interventions as this is seen as the Priest's domain Support client in their spiritual growth and development.

Points about the Clergy

Clergy and religious often seek professional consultation to strengthen their skills in pastoral counseling and psychological intervention as well as to obtain treatment views (Richards & Bergin, 2000). The reasons for treatment may be similar to those of the general population or could be specific to their vocation. Eastern Orthodox requires celibacy among bishops only. The marriage of Orthodox clergy must take place prior to ordination into the priesthood. Married clergy may not become bishops. Women have no clerical function and may not be ordained but can perform auxiliary tasks for the church.

Self Identified Eastern Orthodox
2000
1,500,000 Members
(American Religious Identification Survey, 2000)

Mainline Protestant

Scholars of religion tend to use the term "Mainline Protestant" to enfold the four main denominations of Lutheran, Presbyterian, Episcopal/Anglican, and Methodist traditions. Each tradition includes many sizable churches. For example, the Lutheran Church includes the Lutheran Church in American, The American Lutheran Church, and the Lutheran church – Missouri Synod, and Wisconsin Evangelical Lutheran Synod, each with thousands of participants (Richards & Bergin, 2000). (The Missouri and Wisconsin Synods are the most conservative of the three branches - see Fundamentalism.)

The term "mainline" is used because of they represented a large majority of the early American culture, and are comfortable in contemporary secular culture since they played a part in its creation.

Also included the Congregationalist Church (United Church of Christ), Disciples of Christ, American Baptists, and the Reformed Churches including the Reformed Church of America and the Christian Reformed Church (Richards & Bergin, 2000).

Together the Mainline Protestant traditions welcomes several million adult members nationally (Yearbook of American & Canadian Churches, 2002).

Though there are several distinguishable differences between these traditions, for the purpose of this book they are presented in generalization. All four mainline Protestant denominations support ethnic diversity within their traditions. Specific and pronounced differences in views and beliefs will be presented separately.

<u>Beliefs and Practices</u>
All four main traditions share the following: An optimistic view toward human nature, increased flexibility in the interpretation of scripture and church tradition, avoiding Biblical literalism, openness to scientific discovery and medical and psychological therapies, and less stress on the distinctive traditions of each

denomination (Richards & Bergin, 2000). The Episcopal/Anglican, Lutheran, Presbyterian follow the Nicene Creed and the Apostles Creed as statements of faith.

Specifics Include:
Disciples of Christ – There is no doctrine or dogma beyond the belief in Jesus Christ. Individual interpretation of scripture is highly regarded. A strong objection to matters which divide Christianity.

Episcopal – They appeal to tradition, scriptures, reason, and personal experience to demonstrate their faith as Christians.

Lutheran – Our way of living is a by-product of our way of believing in God's laws. Sin is a basic condition of our personality.

Methodist - A belief in the natural sinfulness of humanity and the need for individual repentance.

Presbyterian - Forgiveness, grace, and salvation are obtained through a direct relationship with God.

United Church of Christ – Physical and spiritual liberation of all human beings is frequently expressed through words and actions

View of Deity
Disciples of Christ – The belief in Jesus as the Christ and acceptance of Him as Lord and personal savior. A general acceptance of the Trinity.

Episcopal – Belief in the Holy Trinity: The Father who is good, infinite and omnipotent, The Son who is Jesus Christ whose life, death and resurrection liberated humanity from sin, and the Holy Spirit who represents God's power of love, and appears in mysterious ways. Jesus is both God and man united in one person for the salvation of mankind.

Lutheran – The Law of God as found for example, in the Ten Commandments, tells what God expects of us and how we are to live. God demands punishment for our disobedience but because of his love and mercy He doesn't want to have anyone punished. We are forgiven through Jesus Christ and given eternal life with God.

Methodist – Belief in the Trinity as God the Father, the Son who is Jesus Christ, and the Holy Spirit who is the empowering spirit of God.

Presbyterian – All must trust in Christ as their forgiving savior and promise to follow Christ and his example for living. God is truth, beauty, intention, purpose, energy and will. God is revealed in Jesus Christ. God is the Lord of conscience. The Old and New Testaments are in infallible rules of faith and practice.

United Church of Christ – Trinitarian belief. Statement of Faith begins: " We believe in God, the Eternal Spirit, Father of our Lord Jesus Christ [...] ." The Holy Spirit is referred to as "creating and renewing the Church [...], binding in covenant faithful people of all ages, tongues, and races." They recognize Jesus Christ as the sole Head of the Church (Rosten, 1975).

View of Afterlife
Disciples of Christ – Some believe in the literal interpretation of heaven and hell, but most leave the details of future rewards and punishments to Divine Mercy.

Episcopal – Man is judged by God at the time of death according to his or her real character. Heaven and Hell are states of mind. Heaven is a state in which service to God is enjoyed. Hell is alienation from God.

Lutheran – The goal is the perfect existence that is obtained through total obedience to God. Those who live and die in faith will live with God eternally, freed from the limits of time and space. Victory over death is the destiny of God's people.

Methodist – Most do not believe in a heaven "up there" and a hell "down there." Heaven is the realm of mind and spirit where the blessed live in the company of God and Jesus Christ. Hell is where God and Jesus Christ are absent.

Presbyterian – Heaven and Hell are actual places as well as states of mind and character. We live in a moral universe where sins carry the appropriate penalty and righteousness the reward of the vision of God.

United Church of Christ – Most do not believe there are specific places of eternal bliss or punishment after death. They do believe God judges men and nation by his righteous will and that he promises eternal life (Rosten, 1975).

Spiritual practices and Healing Traditions
Attending worship services, prayer, spiritual meditation, reading Bible and other spiritual writings, laying on of hands, healing services, and teachings about grace and forgiveness.

Abortion and Birth Control
Abortion is generally discouraged except in cases of rape, extreme fetus abnormalities or danger to the mother's life, though denominations may vary in acceptability. Contraception is accepted in all denominations.

Sexuality
Sexuality is viewed as the highest form of human intimacy. Heterosexual sex within a marriage is viewed as the only legitimate sexual expression of God's love. Sex outside the marriage is discouraged. The stance on homosexual behavior is being debated. It was viewed as immoral with a recent shift toward mutual understanding and tolerance. Presbyterian, Lutheran, and Methodist churches official views are that homosexuality is

against scriptural teachings. Disciples of Christ, United Church of Christ, and the Episcopal Church have taken no official position.

<u>Marriage and Divorce</u>
Marriage is considered a blessing or vocation not a sacrament and is expected to be a lifelong commitment except in Episcopal/Anglican and Lutheran Churches where it is a sacrament. Divorce, remarriage, and single parent families were considered wrong but are now viewed with more tolerance. The remarriage of the innocent party is viewed as acceptable. Disciples of Christ have no central authority speaking on this issue.

<u>Alcohol, Illicit Drugs</u>
Lutherans, Presbyterians, and Episcopalians discourage excessive use of alcohol, tobacco, and other drugs, as well as, gambling. Moderate use of alcohol is tolerated. Methodists disapprove of all use of alcohol and diversions such as gambling.

<u>Medicine</u>
Medication is accepted.
Suicide and euthanasia
Suicide is considered wrong. Physician-assisted suicide is opposed, although there is some acceptance of passive euthanasia, i.e. discontinuation of life support and forgoing of extreme measures to sustain life.

<u>View of Therapy</u>
All tend to have positive views of mental health professions. They have an understanding that physical, spiritual, and mental health is different though interrelated. They are open to psychological, biological, and medical understandings of illness. Some clients might fear therapists would undermine their religious beliefs and values.

<u>Religious-clinical issues</u>
Sexuality, divorce, excessive alcohol or drug use, abortion, and euthanasia.

Assessment Recommendations
Assess clients religious and spiritual functioning and how it might be relevant to their psychological issues, psychosocial functioning, and treatment planning.

Treatment Recommendations
Likely to be comfortable with most secular approaches to therapy. Use interventions that help clients grant forgiveness, seek forgiveness, and feel forgiven. Collaboration with pastoral care centers. Some spiritual interventions may be appropriate but assess whether the client is interested in incorporating spiritual or religious issues into his or her treatment.

Points about the Clergy
Men and women are ordained. Celibacy is not required. There are Episcopal monks and nuns who take the vows of poverty, chastity and obedience, who do not marry, and live in monastic communities.

Self Identified Protestant Members
2000
Disciples of Christ (1974) – 1,335,458. **Episcopal** (1999) – 2,300,461.
Lutheran – 5,125,919. **Methodist** – 8,340,954. **Presbyterian** – 3,485,332.
United Church of Christ (1974) – 1,867,810.
(Yearbook of American and Canadian Churches, 2002)

Specific dates after denomination indicate if the statistics were gathered prior to the 2000 report.

Evangelical and Fundamentalist Protestant

Both the Evangelical and Fundamentalist denominations are largely comprised of churches in the Anabapist tradition. The largest of these is the fundamentalist Southern Baptist Convention with membership over 16 million (Richards & Bergin, 2000). The Lutheran Missouri and Wisconsin Synods also believe in biblical literalism and hold conservative views.

Evangelical and Fundamentalists beliefs can be found within all the mainline Protestant denominations. Generally speaking, the major difference between the mainline Protestants and the Fundamentalists is the latter believes in the literal interpretation of Scripture with no room for deviation. Evangelicals are generally not Fundamentalists though some consider themselves as such.

Beliefs
Evangelical and Fundamentalists have many common beliefs including the belief in the virgin birth, repenting one's sins to become saved, the need to cultivate a personal relationship with Jesus, and viewing the Bible as God's unerring word.
Converts who repent are believed to metaphorically die and resurrect in the name of Jesus Christ thus giving rise to the term "born again Christian."
Fundamentalists and Evangelicals believe they are to evangelize all nations by preaching the gospel (Good News) because they believe Christ will return and will judge all, both living and dead. All unbelievers will be separated from God eternally while all faithful believers will live forever with God in heaven.
Unlike Evangelicals, Fundamentalists believe in separatism from the world to maintain personal holiness and therefore impose strict codes of dress and behavior. Associating with non-believers is frowned upon. They quote the Bible as explicitly prohibiting a believer from entering into any serious relationship or marriage with a non-believer.

- Baptist – Encourages member's personal independence and the right to interpret the New Testament for him/herself in matters of faith and practice.
- Evangelical Presbyterian - Forgiveness, grace, and salvation are obtained through a direct relationship with God. They also believe in the inerrancy of the Bible

Dress Code - Fundamentalists
Strong emphasis on the presentation of purity. Women are forbidden to wear slacks, tight fitting clothes, flashy jewelry, miniskirts, shorts or bikinis. Hair should be worn long. No make-up. Men must wear hair short, no scruffy looking jeans or clothing, and should not wear tight pants.

View of Deity
Trinitarian Belief as God the Father, Jesus Christ is His Son who sacrificed his life to pay for our sins, and the Holy Spirit. The life, teachings and devotional worship of Jesus Christ is central to this tradition. God has omnipotent power.
- Baptist – Most accept the doctrine of the Trinity. Jesus is Lord. The Scriptures are the sole norm for faith and practice, as demonstrated in the New Testament which is full of baptized believers. They also believe in the inerrancy of the Scriptures.

Spiritual practices and Healing Traditions
Regular participation in church services, healing services, and activities. Strong need to redeem the world (evangelize). Shared social support to and from the religious community. They have a heavy emphasis on missionary work. Healthy lifestyle practices such as abstaining from drug use. Prayer and Bible study.

View of After Life
Christ will return and judge all, both living and dead. All unbelievers will be separated from God eternally and all faithful believers will live forever with God in heaven.
Baptist – Most believe in some form of life beyond the grave though there are a range of thoughts and ideas about how that

life would be lived. Some Baptists find the concept of committing sins bad enough in a short (earth) lifetime to warrant an eternal hell, hard to reconcile with a loving God. A general unity is found on moral and social issues. What separates them is the extreme stance Fundamentalists take on issues.

Abortion and Birth Control
Abortion is strongly opposed except is ectopic pregnancy and danger to mother's life. Contraception is accepted.

Sexuality
Premarital, homosexual and extramarital sex is opposed.

Marriage and divorce
Divorce and remarriage is opposed except when the divorce is due to spouse infidelity and abuse. Remarriage is allowed only when the divorce was due to infidelity. Members of the Church can only date and marry other members of the Church. Wives are subservient to their husbands who are considered the head of the household.

Alcohol and Illicit Drugs
Opposed to all alcohol, tobacco, and drug use. Some Fundamentalists also oppose dancing, swearing/cursing, and gambling.

Medicine
Use of medicine is accepted.

Suicide and Euthanasia
Both are wrong.

Religious-clinical issues
Authority figure fights and conflict, corporal punishment, unhealthy group dependency, perfectionism, gender role issues, excessive guilt and shame, low self-esteem, disillusionment, anger, and rigidity and dogmatism. Evangelical – overt rebelliousness, covert rebellion, or extreme attempts to please. Long term

exposure to toxic messages including don't talk, feel, trust, or want (Sloat, 1990). Fundamentalist – "fundamentalist mindset" including being an absolutist, authoritarian, intolerant, and compulsive about control" (Yao, 1987).

<u>View of Therapy</u>
Both share the fear of therapy eroding their core beliefs, that the therapist will not understand and criticize their beliefs, that will never be whole again, and the fear of accessing the darker sides of their natures (Richards & Bergin, 2000).
But Evangelical and Fundamentalists differ on their views of the mental health profession. Evangelicals generally accept the mental health field though they are more likely to seek psychological support from their pastor or a Christian Counselor. If they are referred for therapy they will actively seek a likeminded therapist. Fundamentalists are suspicious of the mental health field and will most likely to seek psychological support from their pastor or church elder who will admonish members who seek counseling from anyone other than themselves.

<u>Assessment Recommendations</u>
Fundamentalist may not be open to psychological or religious assessments, although Evangelicals are likely to be. A number of psychospiritual measures may be useful for assessment purposes, for example using the Spiritual Themes and Religious Responses Test by Saur and Saur (1990).

<u>Treatment Recommendations</u>
To build trust and credibility a suggestion is to work within their idioms or religious language. Many secular theories and approaches to therapy have some value. Rogerian person-centered therapy is more readily accepted. A variety of spiritual interventions may be helpful, including forgiveness, prayer, personal feelings, examining internalized image of God, and challenging distorted religious beliefs. Consult with religious leaders.

Self Identified Evangelical and Fundamentalist Protestants
2000
5,125,919 Members

Self Identified Southern Baptist – Self Identified Baptist
(other than Southern) – 3,500,000
15,960,308 Members
(Yearbook of American and Canadian Churches, 2002)

Pentecostal/Charismatic

The Pentecostal/Charismatic Movement grew out of the Evangelical and Fundamentalist traditions. They have not been included in the above denominations because of the Pentecostal's specific manifestation of "Gifts of the Spirit" such as prophesizing and speaking in tongues (Wright, 1994). Included here is the Assemblies of God Church, one of the largest denomination of Pentecostal groups with over 30 million members. Charismatic is a more contemporary term for the Pentecostal Movement.

Beliefs
Pentecostal and Charismatic core beliefs are found in scripture and in the use of the Holy Bible. Main core beliefs are that Jesus forgives and saves from sin those who believe in Him (Holy bible, John 1:12, 3:16 – 17, 1:7-9). Jesus is physically coming again to reign over this earth (Holy Bible, Revelation 19:11-20:4). Jesus is mankind's only savior (Holy Bible, Mark 16:15).
Pentecostals emphasize spiritual experience, one such experience is speaking in tongues. The Bible is the literal inerrant book inspired by God.

View of Deity
Trinitarian belief of God the Father, Jesus Christ is the Son of God, and the Holy Spirit. Jesus is the central focus of worship and that God is totally revealed in Jesus Christ. God speaks to individual believers as well as to the entire church. Salvation occurs when there is an acceptance Christ as Savior. Those Baptized in the Holy Spirit are empowered to witness Christ.

View of Afterlife
Accountability and ultimate judgement of all human beings: believers for their works and unbelievers for their sins and the survival of the spirit and soul to live in either everlasting life or everlasting damnation (Holy Bible, Corinthians 3:10 – 15).

Abortion and Birth Control

Abortion is opposed except for ectopic pregnancies or danger to the mother's life. Contraception for married couples is accepted.

Children

All Pentecostal/Charismatic groups oppose any mistreatment of children that could be classified and physical, emotional or sexual abuse.

Sexuality

Sexuality is viewed as a sacred gift from God and should be celebrated only in marriage because God designed such for the happiness, well-being, protection, and stability in the life of each person, the family, and the human community. Homosexual behavior is seen as unnatural and contrary to Scripture. Assemblies of God opposes homosexuality and the gay lifestyle which are considered sinful.

Marriage and Divorce

Marriage is valued. Divorce and remarriage is strongly discouraged although varying opinions exist. Divorce may be granted because of the repeated adultery of a partner, abuse, and abandonment. The innocent party is not bound by the former marriage and is free to remarry. Wives are subservient to their husbands who are considered the head of the household.

Alcohol, Illicit Drugs

Drunkenness and drug abuse in any form are opposed. Many Pentecostals encourage total abstinence from alcohol, but some Charismatic churches accept moderate use.

Medicine

Use of medicine is accepted

Suicide and Euthanasia

Both are opposed.

View of Therapy

Tend to view behavioral sciences with suspicion and oppose any kind of therapy that is not strictly biblical. Assemblies of God states if the counselor does not believe one can have a personal relationship with God, and instead approaches life strictly from a humanistic point of view, the advice and counseling approach will be devoid of an essential component of true healing—God. Therefore, it's best to choose a counselor who is a Christian (Assemblies of God, 2003).

Spiritual practices and Healing Traditions

Participation in church service and activities. Prayer and Bible study. Prayer for sick and miracles of healing for the body, soul, and spirit. The belief that the death of Jesus Christ made possible physical, spiritual, and emotional healing with the recognition that God often uses doctors and counselors in administering healing. Faith in Christ is the link to God's divine healing power.

Religious-clinical issues

Overly harsh, punitive images of God. Religiously based guilt, anger, anxiety, depression, and perfectionism in belief expression. Poor self-image or self-esteem. Tend to have mood related disorders (Parziale, 2003). Gender role issues. Inhibited sexuality and sexual guilt. Difficulties with forgiveness, divorce and remarriage, relationship issues with non-believer.

Assessment recommendations

Explore the role and importance of the client's religious faith. Inquire about client's religious background and current beliefs about their church and God.

Treatment Recommendations

Do not use psychological interventions that are contrary to Pentecostal scriptural understandings. Prayer, use of scriptural teachings and stories, and consulting with clergy may be helpful interventions.

Self Identified Pentecostals (1998) - 1,500,000 Members
Self Identified Assemblies of God – (2000) 1,506,835 Members
(Yearbook of American and Canadian Churches, 2002)

Church of Jesus Christ of Latter-Day Saints (LDS) – Mormon

In 1820 a then fifteen year old Joseph Smith saw, heard and experienced a Divine vision and declaration to restore the Gospel of Jesus Christ. Joseph Smith is looked upon by his followers as a prophet of God and is the founder of the LDS movement. Since the time of Joseph Smith the LDS Church has always looked to Prophets, Seers, or Revelators to stand as the head of the church. LDS believe that affairs of the Church are directed by Jesus Christ through the church leaders.

Beliefs
Beliefs are similar to Orthodox Christian ideas but diverge at the LDS teaching that God is omniscient *and* has a physical body. Through repentance and baptism anyone can gain entrance to Christ's earthly kingdom. They believe they are literally the children of God with Divine potential (Romans, 8:16). Men and women are equal in the eyes of the Lord and cannot achieve the highest eternal rewards without each other. Both faith and works are essential to salvation.

View of Deity
Trinitarian belief in God the Father, His Son Jesus Christ, and the Holy Ghost. Revelation from God didn't cease at the crucifixion of Jesus but has continued through the ages through prophets. They worship Jesus Christ and His Gospel.

View of Afterlife
After death the spirit goes to the "spirit world" to learn and repent. Judgement occurs on the basis of earthly desire, intentions, actions, choices in life, and the willing acceptance of Jesus Christ as Savior. After judgement the soul attains one of three heavenly kingdoms, each with varying degrees of blessedness. Heaven is considered a place where loved one's, family and friends are united after death. Those who are indifferent to their opportunities on earth

will suffer from the knowledge that they have fallen short of their highest possible happiness and will endure "hell" in the hereafter.

Abortion and Birth Control
Abortion is vigorously condemned except in cases of rape, incest and danger to the mother's life. Contraception is accepted though child bearing is preferred.

Sexuality
Sexual relations between husband and wife are considered beautiful and sacred. Premarital, homosexual, masturbation and extramarital sex are considered sinful.

Marriage and Divorce
Marriage is a holy union intended to last for eternity. The Mormon believes there can be no heaven without his family. Only Temple marriages are believed to be binding after death. Civil marriages are not binding. Divorce is strongly discouraged although the church grants divorces based on infidelity, abuse and severe incompatibility. Remarriage is accepted. Polygamy, once practiced by a minority of Mormon's, is grounds for excommunication from the church. Wives are subservient to their husbands who are considered the head of the household.

Alcohol and Illicit Drugs
Any use of alcohol, illicit drugs, tobacco, coffee, and tea is considered sinful. Complete abstinence from these substances is the norm.

Medicine
Use of medication in accepted

Suicide and Euthanasia
Suicide is considered against God's will. Active euthanasia is morally unacceptable, although passive euthanasia is acceptable is certain circumstances.

View of Therapy

Tend to have fairly positive views of the mental health professions, although considerable distrust of "secular" psychotherapy exists. There are many Church/LDS owned mental health facilities. Most members tend to prefer working with same faith therapists.

Spiritual practices and Healing Traditions

Worship services, temple ordinances and services, prayer, scripture study, family home evenings, blessings including the laying on of hands, fasting, channeling spirits for guidance, church and humanitarian service, hymns, partaking of sacraments, baptism, family history work genealogy).

Religious-clinical issues

Perfectionism, shame, authority conflicts and abuses, sexual guilt and inhibition, denial of anger and conflict, masturbation, gender role conflict and sexism, social conformity and pressure.

Assessment Recommendations

Assess client's degree of involvement with the religious community and to what degree religious beliefs and involvement are positive or negative influences. Other religious dimensions may also be relevant to assess (see Spiritual Assessment Guide).

Treatment Recommendations

Variety of psychological and spiritual interventions could be appropriate, including teaching spiritual concepts, spiritual self-disclosure, and prayer. Therapeutic techniques that work best include those containing goal oriented action, and self-reliance Consulting with client's religious leaders can often be helpful.

Incongruent interventions include: sex therapies involving sex outside the marriage including masturbation, group therapies requiring high levels of self disclosure or emotional venting (12 step groups or standard group therapy not included), feminist therapies, gay affirmation therapies, some of the rational-emotive therapies that call for a denouncement of authority figures, and long term analytical approaches (Richards & Bergin, 2000).

Self Identified Jesus Christ of Latter Day Saints – (2000)
5,208,827 Members
(Yearbook of American and Canadian Churches, 2002)

Janine d'Haven

Seventh Day Adventist

Beliefs
A Seventh Day Adventist has accepted Christ as his personal Savior and walks in humble obedience to the will of God as reveled in Holy Scripture. They believe the Bible literally. They seek patterns in their lives according to teachings of the Bible. They believe it is their duty to warn mankind that the end of the world is at hand. They believe God created the earth literally in six days and that the first chapter in Genesis is fact. They observe the Sabbath on Saturday not Sunday.

View of Deity
Seventh Day Adventists believe in the Trinity and reverently worship Father, Son and Holy Spirit as three persons in one God.

Spiritual practices and Healing Traditions
Sabbath-day observance, worshipping, social support, prayer, scripture study, baptism and laying on of hands. Healthy lifestyle behaviors such as "clean" meats, strict kosher and/or vegetarian diets are encouraged, as well as, abstinence from alcohol and drug use.

View of Afterlife
There is no eternal life apart from Christ. Only Christ can make humans immortal. But immortality will not be conferred until the resurrection at the second coming of Christ.

Abortion and birth control
Abortion is condemned except in cases of rape, incest, or the endangerment of the mother's health. Contraception is accepted.

Sexuality
Premarital, homosexual, and extramarital sex are considered wrong.

Marriage and Divorce
Marriage is regarded as a divinely established institution. Divorce and remarriage are discouraged except in cases of adultery.

Alcohol and Illicit Drugs
Abstinence from alcohol, drugs and tobacco use is required. Drinking caffeinated coffee or tea is discouraged.

Medicine
Use of medication is accepted.

Suicide and Euthanasia
Suicide and euthanasia are considered morally wrong. Passive euthanasia may be acceptable in certain circumstances.

View of Therapy
Members, especially conservative ones, may distrust mental health professionals and prefer therapy from Christian therapist.

Religious-clinical issues
Perfectionism, authority issues, sexual inhibitions, projection and anger, fear of dependency on the therapist, guilt and shame, victimization, depression, and patriarchal attitudes toward women in gender roles.

Assessment Recommendations
Do not use psychological assessments that may appear unsympathetic toward religious persons. Several spiritual assessment measures may be helpful.

Treatment Recommendations
Relaxation training, rational-emotive therapy, Transactional Analysis, and Rogerian therapy can be helpful. Child, marriage, and family counseling are accepted (Richards & Bergin, 2000).

Points about the Clergy

Clergy burnout, depression, tendencies toward perfectionism, needing to be the "super clergy", morale issues especially in the pastor-spouse relationship, trouble setting priorities and saying "no".

Self Identified Seventh Day Adventist
2000
880,921 Members
(Yearbook of American and Canadian Churches, 2002)

Christian Scientist – Science of Mind

The Church of Christ, Scientist, has been defined by its founder, Mary Baker Eddy, as "a Church designed to commemorate the word and works of our Master, which should reinstate primitive Christianity and its lost element of healing" (Rosten, 1975). Christian Scientists do not celebrate holidays.

Beliefs
God is the Divine Mind, the source and substance of man's true being. Mind and spirit are cause - man and the universe are effect. Imperfection of every sort belongs to a mortal, material sense of existence. Matter is only a false sense of substance. To the extent that an individual understands his true selfhood to be spiritual rather that material, he is able to follow the example of Christ in overcoming the ills and evils of the flesh (Rosten, L).

View of Deity
Christ is the true idea of God. As Son of God He is eternally present to redeem humanity from sin, disease, and death. Christ's works are not considered miracles but the understanding of divine natural law. The Trinity is seen as Life, Truth, and Love. Jesus is the highest expression of the Christ. God created man in his image.

Spiritual practices and Healing Traditions
Health is a spiritual reality not a physical condition. True health is eternal. Healing includes healing broken hearts, minds, homes, sick bodies, and is directly applicable to all of societies ills.

View of Afterlife
Death is not seen as the termination of an individual's life but as a phase in the belief that life is material. Death doesn't effect man's eternal existence and eventually each individual must recognize his immortal life. Heaven and Hell are considered states of being and not future dwellings.

Abortion and Birth Controll
Birth Control is the responsibility of each couple who are free to follow their own judgement as to having children and how many. Abortion involving operations or drugs is incompatible with Christian Science belief.

Sexuality
All forms of random or deviant sexuality are calling for specific healing rather than for condemnation.

Marriage and Divorce
The Church is run by lay clergy, therefore there is no one to perform a legal ceremony. Civil ceremonies are suggested. No official position on divorce though Christian Science practitioners are available to help individuals find healing through prayer regarding such problems as infidelity, sterility, indifference, and abuse (First Church of Christ Scientist, 2003).

Alcohol and Illicit Drugs
Addictive or intoxicating substances can enslave individuals. Substance use is highly discouraged.

Medicine
Christian Scientist may employ a physician and is free to choose medication, though many will rely on their faith to heal.

Suicide and Euthanasia
"We are strengthened to face any temptation of suicide with Christly courage" (First Church of Christ Scientist, 2003). They hold a belief that one can defeat suggestions of suicide by acknowledging his or her own Godlike nature as true and *expressing it.* Euthanasia in not generally an issue since life support or other means of medical intervention would probably not be employed.

View of Therapy
They do not accept the effectiveness of the study of the human mind or psyche. Christian Science is based on the understanding

of the Divine Mind or Soul. Therefore a member of this community will not seek therapy.

The number of Members is not recorded.

Unitarian Universalist

The community of Unitarian Universalists freely chooses their ethics and beliefs, which are constantly evolving through out their lives. Their churches are organized as free religious communities in which they can unite for the celebration of life, for sharing values, for service and for comfort – without having to accept a dogmatic creed (Rosten, 1975). The term "Unitarian", is from the sixteenth century and speaking about those who denied the doctrine of the trinity. "Universalist" stands for the teaching that salvation was not for a limited few, but is a gift to all from God.

Beliefs
Unitarians believe in the worth of all human beings. Each individual must decide for themselves about God. They recognize their responsibility to help create a just and peaceful social order for all peoples. They believe that significant meaning and value can be discovered in life on earth without necessarily affirming a life after death. They also believe in the principles of freedom, trusting that a free society provides the maximum opportunity for all persons to find and enjoy the good life. Human beings have a responsibility not only for their own behavior but to help create a society that doesn't breed crime, corruption, and brutality (Rosten, 1975).

View of Deity
They believe in the oneness of reality and think of God as a unity rather than a trinity. They believe everyone is Divine. They are inspired by the life of Jesus.

Spiritual practices and Healing Traditions
Meditation with the expression of one's aspirations is the main form of prayer. Services are dedicated to the lives of their members and are celebrations focused on the children, coming of age, marriages, and in remembrance of the dead.

View of Afterlife
Heaven and hell are considered states of mind created by human beings and not actual places. Hell is created by injustice, violence, tyranny, and war. Heaven is created by compassion, mercy, liberty, and love (Rosten, 1975).

Abortion and Birth Control
Strong advocates for responsible parenthood and in conceiving only the those children who will be loved, wanted and cared for. Abortion is an ethical matter left up to the individual woman.

Sexuality
Sex is considered beautiful and profound. They believe that sexual activity, performed privately between two consenting adults should not be subjected to legal sanctions (Rosten, 1975). They are opposed to all discrimination against homosexuals.

Marriage and Divorce
Marriage is the unifying of lives, love and happiness and should be entered into freely. The decision to divorce is entirely up to the persons involved.

Alcohol and Illicit Drugs
No official position on this subject though for spiritual purposes moderation in the use of alcohol is probably encouraged. Use of illicit and addictive drugs is discouraged.

Medicine
Accept the use medications

Suicide and Euthanasia
No official position on this subject. However with the belief that all life is precious and their strong pacifist stance suicide is most likely not thought of as an option to resolving issues. Passive euthanasia is probably accepted. Though medically assisted suicide is not acceptable

View of Therapy
Acceptance of the value of therapy and not opposed to counseling.

Religious-clinical issues
Due to the high value placed on individual responsibility, specific religious clinical issues would not apply.

Assessment Recommendations
They have a high level of comfort with therapeutic interventions and modalities. Open to the inclusion of spiritual interventions and exploration.

Treatment Recommendations
Treatment recommendations based on assessments and presenting issues. No specific treatment recommendations

Self Identified Unitarian Universalists
2000
220,000 Members
(Yearbook of American and Canadian Churches, 2002)

Religious Society of Friends –Quaker

A Quaker is a member of the Religious Society of Friends, who hold the belief that there is "that of God in everyone." The term "Quaker" was a nickname given to the followers of George Fox in the seventeenth century when Fox had told a magistrate to tremble at the word of God. Quakerism began as a protest against the religious hierarchy, the domination or the church by the state, excessive formalism in religious doctrine and elaborate rituals in religious ceremonies (Rosten, 1975). They have formed simple, silent, gatherings to honor God as the essence of their worship.

Beliefs
There are a variety of beliefs and forms of worship in American Quakerism. One basic belief is that God is in everyone. God speaks to all through the still, small inner voice. The purpose of life is to hear and obey the Lord who is Jesus Christ. The central belief is in immediate and continuous revelation available to all who are seriously seek it, in all times and places. Quakers are strongly opposed to war and are advocates for non-violence and peace.

View of Deity
God can be approached and experienced by each individual directly. No intermediary   (i.e. Priest, Minister, etc) is necessary. God is experienced through "Inner Light", which is the spirit of "Christ Within." From this contact, God's will is determined, direction is given for all human affairs, and the power to live the abundant life is shared. This is a universal grace (Rosten, 1975).

Spiritual practices and Healing Traditions
Meetings of Worship is a service with no fixed agenda, ritual, or minister. Gatherings are done in silence. Through the silence spiritual messages such as prayers can be shared. Worship is under the direct guidance of the Holy Spirit.

View of Afterlife
What occurs after death is up to individual interpretation. Most emphasize that the "kingdom is now" making inquiries into the afterlife unnecessary. Many hold diverse views concerning life after death.

Abortion and Birth Control
Birth control is up to the individual. There is no formal position on abortion.

Sexuality
Quaker opinion is that too much emphasis is placed on sex whether it is "straight" or "gay." There is no formal opinion on homosexuality.

Marriage and Divorce
Love is the only appropriate reason for marriage. Since there aren't ordained clergy, a the bride and groom "marry each other" in the presence of God with friends and family as witnesses. Marriage is a partnership of equals. Divorce was historically strongly opposed, but doesn't face the same intense opposition as it had in former years.

Alcohol and Illicit Drugs
No official position on this subject though for spiritual purposes, moderation in the use of alcohol is probably encouraged. Use of illicit and addictive drugs is discouraged.

Medicine
Acceptance of the use of medications

Suicide and Euthanasia
No formal position regarding this subject. Though with the belief that all life is precious and their strong pacifist stance suicide is most likely not thought of as an option to resolving issues. Passive euthanasia is probably accepted. Though medically assisted suicide is not acceptable.

View of Therapy
Acceptance of the value of therapy and not opposed to counseling.

Religious-clinical issues
Due to the high value placed on individual responsibility, specific religious clinical issues would not apply.

Assessment Recommendations
They have a high level of comfort with therapeutic interventions and modalities. Open to the inclusion of spiritual interventions and exploration.

Treatment Recommendations
Treatment recommendations based on assessments and presenting issues. No specific treatment recommendations

Self Identified Quakers
2000
134, 000 Members

Jehovah's Witnesses

The name Jehovah's Witnesses is found in the Bible (Isaiah 43:12) "Ye are my witnesses, saith Jehovah, and I am God." They have no creed but follow the Bible. They feel the Bible is entirely consistent and practical for our lives today. They are God's servants. They do not celebrate religious holidays nor pay homage to any unchristian image (i.e. American Flag). Jehovah's Witness preach in homes, door to door, on street corners, etc. because Jesus did and they are following his example.

Beliefs
Jehovah is the one true God whose sovereignty has been challenged by Satan in the Garden of Eden. God's primary purpose is to regain sovereign rule. He sent Jesus to earth to provide the ransom sacrifice and to lay the foundation for God's new system (Rosten, 1975). When Christ came to earth it marked the beginning of the end for Satan on earth. In the coming "great tribulation" God will destroy all the wickedness on earth including the Devil, and will mark the thousand-year reign of Christ.

View of Deity
Jehovah's Witnesses believe that Jehovah God and Jesus Christ are two distinct persons and are not combined with the "Holy Ghost." They do believe, however, that the Holy Spirit is God's active force.

Spiritual practices and Healing Traditions
Baptism by total body immersion is a symbol of dedication to Jehovah. Attending regular congregational meetings, prayer meetings, and Bible study. Preach the words of Jehovah door to door and in public. They govern their activities in accord with God's word.

View of Afterlife
Hell is the grave and not a place of eternal torment. Hell is a place of rest in hope of resurrection. Heaven is inhabited by

spirit creatures and God's throne. The reward for a spiritual life is heaven on earth. After the great tribulation only 144,00 will go to heaven, which means they will live in an earthly paradise. Graves will be resurrected and those who prove obedient to God will be offered the opportunity to live forever.

Abortion and Birth Control
Birth control is an individual matter.   Jehovah's Witnesses condemn abortion.

Sexuality
Premarital sex, adultery, bestiality, incest and homosexuality are all serious sins against God.
If an unmarried couple is living together they must separate or get married. Only heterosexual's are permitted to be members. (Leviticus 18:6, Romans 1:26-27, Corinthians 6:9, Awake, 2003).

Marriage and Divorce
View marriage as a sacred vow made before God.   It seals a permanent union that can be broken only by infidelity or death. In marriage a husband should love his wife as he does himself (Magida, 1996). Divorce may only be obtained on the grounds of adultery or any kind of sexual relations outside of the marriage. If a member is divorced for any other reason and remarries, they are expelled from the congregation.

Alcohol and Illicit Drugs
Alcohol in moderation is tolerated but heavy drinking is wrong in the eyes of God. Gambling is tainted by greed and any form of gambling including lotteries, bingo, etc. are forbidden (Awake, 2003).

Medicine
While there is a reluctant acceptance of some medications, blood transfusions are prohibited. Only blood substitute can be used.

Suicide and Euthanasia
Life is sacred to God. Any attempt to end a life is a sin against God.

View of Therapy
Jehovah's Witnesses do not officially promote or recommend any specific form of therapy, be it medical or psychiatric. They do not endorse therapy though each member can research therapy and weigh the implications of any treatment against beliefs and form their own decision.

Religious-clinical issues
Overly harsh, punitive images of God. Religiously based guilt, anger, anxiety, depression, and perfectionism in belief expression, and poor self-image or self-esteem, inhibited sexuality and sexual guilt. Difficulties with forgiveness, divorce and remarriage, relationship issues with non-believers. Many who leave the faith are given an exit interview and counseling about why they have left and how they are adjusting to life outside of the faith. This could increase anxiety, depression, fear and anger.

Assessment Recommendations
If you have the opportunity to counsel a Jehovah's Witness do not use psychological assessments that may appear unsympathetic toward religious persons. Several spiritual assessment measures may be helpful. Assess client's degree of involvement with the religious community and to what degree religious beliefs and involvement are positive or negative influences. Other religious dimensions may also be relevant to assess (see Spiritual Assessment Guide).

Treatment Recommendations
To build trust and credibility a suggestion is to work within their idioms or religious language. Many secular theories and approaches to therapy have some value. Rogerian person-centered therapy is more readily accepted. A variety of spiritual interventions may be helpful, including forgiveness, prayer, personal feelings, examining

internalized image of God, and challenging assessed distorted religious beliefs. Consult with religious leaders.

Self Identified Jehovah's Witnesses
2000
998,166 Members
(Yearbook of American and Canadian Churches, 2002)

Judaism

It is easy to trace the origins of Judaism back four thousand years to Abraham, the first Hebrew to receive a revelation from God. The source of the word "Jew" is from the Hebrew word "yehudi" meaning members of the tribe of Judah. The Jewish people have an extraordinary history of endurance, survival, faith, and community fellowship. Only the Jews have had their homeland destroyed twice, have been dispersed throughout the world (Diaspora) leaving them homeless, have endured unparalleled hatred where ever they have lived, and have survived the most systematic attempt in history (except for Gypsies) to destroy an entire people. They can claim the honor of having their four thousand-year-old culture survive intact (Prager & Telushkin, 1981).

In an article in Harper's Magazine dated September 1899, Mark Twain expressed Jewish endurance by writing,

> "The Egyptian, the Babylonian, and the Persian rose, filled the planet with sound and splendor, then faded to dreamstuff and passed away; the Greek and the Roman followed and made a vast noise, and they are gone; [...]. The Jew saw them all, beat them all, and is now what he always was, exhibiting no decadence, no infirmities of age, no weakening of his parts, no slowing of his energies, no dulling of his alert and aggressive mind. All things are mortal but the Jew: all other forces pass, but he remains. What is the secret of his immortality?"

Judaism is a nationality, religion, culture and way of life. Community is extremely important. And though the Jewish tradition has broadened over millennia to include Orthodox, Conservative and Reform Judaism, there remains certain underlying foundational beliefs that support all three branches of contemporary Judaism.

The foundational texts of Judaism are known as the Torah, or Pentateuch, or the Five Books of Moses. Christians refer to the

Torah as the Old Testament of the Bible. Judaism has several other important texts including the Talmud and the Mishna.

The following includes commonly held views by the three main branches of Judaism, Orthodox, Conservative, and Reform. When they diverge, views will be presented individually.

Common Beliefs

Judaism emphasizes deed over creed and is an action oriented tradition with the Jewish law as the guiding influence over deeds. Jewish law is extensive consisting of 613 mitzvot (commandments) including the Ten Commandments revealed to Moses on Mt. Sinai. The ultimate purpose of the Laws is to produce good people. Judaism emphasizes right action as it will bring justice. Sin (*chet*) means to "miss the mark" requiring corrective action.

Common View of Deity

Jews hold a common belief that they are bound by a covenant (agreement) to God. They view God as one God "the Lord alone," creator of the universe and who created humans in his own image though not identically. God is portrayed with masculine attributes. He is unchangeable, eternal, transcendent and accessible. Jews use different terms to refer to God including Elohim, Yahweh, and Adonai. The characteristics of God are described by what God is not as opposed to what God is as He is infinite.

View of Afterlife

Jews believe in the immortality of the soul, and immortality whose nature is known only to God. They do not accept the literal interpretation of heaven and hell but believe that each individual receives the judgement they deserve. Orthodox Jews forbid cremation as it destroys the body which is created in the likeness of God.

Orthodox Judaism

Orthodox Jews hold to direct, verbatim revelation of the Torah with strict observance of the 613 mitzvot.

Spiritual practices and Healing Traditions
Study of the Torah, Mishna, and Talmud. Prayer spoken aloud, silently, sung or chanted. Worship in Synagogues. Rituals serve as a way to transmit values and beliefs. Observing biblical holidays and associated rituals such as Rosh Hashanah, Yom Kippur, Passover, Sukkot, and observing mitzvot (the commandments). Celebration of the Sabbath on Saturday. Sabbath is a day of rest, reflection, and time to spend with family. No work or machinery is to be used, and all preparations for the Sabbath are completed before sundown of Friday night. Sabbath is from sundown Friday to sundown Saturday. There is gender separation during worship and requirements to wear the prayer shawl and yarmulke.

Dietary Laws
Kashrut, or keeping Kosher, grew out of the insistence of moral treatment of animals. Three main aspects to keeping Kosher are: only allowed to eat certain species or animal or fish, the slaughter of animals must be done in a certain way to minimize the animals pain, and the forbidding of mixing meat and dairy products at a meal.

Abortion and Birth Control
Abortion is a grave sin except when the mother's life is in danger and during the first 40 days of pregnancy when a rabbi may sanction it. Contraception is generally not permitted unless a medical condition or emotional well-being is in jeopardy.

Sexuality
A positive view of sex within a marriage. Marriage is a mitzvot and is held in high esteem. Intercourse is allowed only at certain times of the month, and is forbidden during menstruation. Premarital, homosexual, and extramarital sex are considered sinful. Male

homosexual behavior is considered a much greater offense that female homosexual behavior. Circumcision is necessary.

Marriage and Divorce
Marriage and having children is considered "mitzvah" – commandment or good deed. Divorce is permitted but not considered lightly. Remarriage is encouraged. Religious affiliation is through the mother. Conversion to the Jewish faith is discouraged. Genders have specific and separate roles. Women are superior in the home while men are superior in the public domain. Women are segregated during worship. The family is the main unit of worship.

Alcohol and Illicit Drugs
Using alcohol in moderation is permissible. Illegal drug use is considered reprehensible. Smoking tobacco is discouraged. A variety of dietary laws are adhered to.

Medicine
Most see no problem with taking psychotropic medication.

Suicide and Euthanasia
Suicide is forbidden. Euthanasia is also forbidden, although passive euthanasia may be circumstantially acceptable.

View of Therapy
Some Orthodox Jews are reluctant to seek therapy because they fear it will conflict with their values.

Religious-clinical issues
Marital discord, sexual problems, intimacy issues, fears of homosexuality, masturbation, feelings of spiritual inadequacy, interfaith marriage, and spiritual identity crises, depression, gender issues, paranoia, enmeshment and boundary issues, anger, and feelings of guilt.

Janine d'Haven

Assessment Recommendations
Assessing the degree of client's religious commitment and observance may be helpful, and whether it is authentic or neurotic.

Treatment Recommendations
Psychodynamic therapy may be viewed with distrust by some, but valued by others. Some spiritual interventions may be helpful such as discussing religious concepts. Consulting with rabbis may be helpful. Because few of the mitzvot are explained, Jews take on the task to interpret the Torah through study, argument and debate. Debate is a traditional part of study and is a customary form of communication and intellectual exploration and will probably occur in therapy (Richards & Bergin, 2000).

Conservative and Reform Judaism

Reform Judaism founded in the late 18th early 19th century grew in response to the human condition and life within a more diverse population. Conservative Judaism is the middle road between Reform and Orthodox practices finding Reform practices to dramatic yet agreeing with the need to adapt to changing times. A major difference between Orthodox and the Reform and Conservative views is that the former interprets Jewish law literally while the latter interpret the law symbolically allowing for greater latitude in understanding, belief and personal choice (Richards & Bergin, 2000). The Torah is divinely inspired rather than revealed verbatim.

Spiritual practices and Healing Traditions
Study of the Torah, Mishna, and Talmud. Prayer and worship. Rituals serve as a way to transmit values and beliefs. Observing biblical holidays and associated ceremonies such as Rosh Hashanah, Yom Kippur, Passover, Sukkot, and observing mitzvot (the commandments). Some Reform Jews celebrate Sabbath on Sunday. There is no gender separation. No requirements to wear the prayer shawl or yarmulke.

Dietary Laws
A variety of dietary laws (keeping Kosher) may or may not be observed.

Abortion and Birth Control
Abortion to preserve the life or health of the mother is permissible. Abortion for frivolous purposes is not acceptable, though this isn't interpreted with rigor. Contraception is acceptable.

Sexuality
Lawful sexuality is a gift and joy. Premarital sex is largely a matter of personal choice. Adultery and incest are forbidden. Male homosexual behavior is prohibited, but the law is silent about

female behavior. Circumcision is debatable but common and usual.

Marriage and Divorce
Marriage and children are highly valued, but divorce is accepted and easy to arrange. Remarriage is encouraged. Religious affiliation could be through the mother or father. Conversion to the Jewish faith is accepted. Men and women have more equality in the home and in public. Women can fully participate in synagogue worship and leadership.   Interfaith marriage is resisted by Conservative Jews, but is more acceptable with Reform Jews.

Alcohol and Illicit drugs
Alcohol in moderation is viewed as a gift from God. Drunkenness is not acceptable.

Medicine
Most see no problem with taking psychotropic medication.

Suicide and Euthanasia
Suicide and euthanasia are not acceptable, although passive euthanasia may be acceptable.

View of Therapy
Most Conservative and Reform Jews are familiar and comfortable with therapy. They may be especially drawn to psychoanalysis. They may be quicker to trust a Jewish therapist but are open to therapy with non-Jews.

Religious-clinical issues
Identity conflicts, depression, paranoia, anger, intellectual identification, guilt and inappropriate feelings of responsibility, intermarriage, and family enmeshment and boundary issues, marital discord, fears of homosexuality, feelings of spiritual inadequacy, and spiritual identity crises.

Assessment Recommendations

Debate and argument should not necessarily be interpreted as resistance. May be helpful to ask clients to explain cultural aspects of their lives. Assess client's religious identity. Separate traditional religious behaviors from neuroses.

Treatment Recommendations

Psychodynamic and other cognitively oriented approaches may be most accepted. Debate, discussion, and argument may be appropriate. Consulting rabbis and other knowledgeable people can be helpful. Because few of the mitzvot are explained, Jews take on the task to interpret the Torah through study, argument and debate. Debate is a traditional part of study and is a customary form of communication and intellectual exploration and will probably occur in therapy (Richards & Bergin, 2000).

Self Identified Members of Judaism
2,831,000 Members
(American Religious Identity Survey, 2001)

Islam

The word "Islam" generally means peace that comes from surrendering to the one true God. The religion of Islam is practiced by Muslims. The prophet Muhammad (referred to as "the Prophet") was born in approximately 570 CE in Mecca. As an adult he occasionally sought solitude in the hills and caves surrounding his village. In or around the year 610 CE he began to experience unusual auditory and visual experiences. He eventually came to understand he was experiencing a revelation from the Arch Angel Gabriel. He then realized that he was meant to communicate his divine revelations to his fellow Meccans. His revelations were intended to set straight the misinterpretations of earlier revelations given through the prophets of the Jews and Christians. Muslims consider Muhammad to be the last of the prophets. Muhammad never claimed to be a miracle worker even though the Qu'ran (also spelled Koran), the Muslim sacred scripture, is considered a miracle and was divinely communicated through Muhammad.

Upon Muhammad's death Muslims had to decide his successor to lead the community. One group claimed the Prophet had designated his cousin and son-in-law as his successor. This group has become known as the Shi'a or Shi'ites. Another group claimed that the Prophets successor should be chosen from among the community of elders. This group has become known as the Sunni Muslims.

Beliefs
The essential beliefs are found in the statement, "I confess that there is no deity but God, and that Muhammad is the Messenger of God." Muslims believe that there is only one transcendent, absolute, Supreme Being called Allah (which means deity) who is above all other spiritual and worldly powers. Muslims also believe that humans know about the Supreme Being because of the prophets. Muslims practice adherence to the Five Pillars of Faith which are: 1- the profession of belief in Allah as the only

God and Muhammad as his prophet, 2- ritual prayer five time per day – dawn, noon, afternoon, sunset, and evening, 3- giving alms to the poor, 4- fasting from dawn till dusk during the holy month of Ramadan, 5- and making the pilgrimage (hajj) to the holy city of Mecca at least once during their lifetime. Muslims adhere to a literal interpretation of scripture.

View of Deity
Muslims describe Allah as the one God, and transcendent. They believe Allah creates life and causes death. Muslims speak of Allah primarily through the "Ninety-Nine Beautiful Names" which include "compassionate" and "merciful."

Clothing
Most items of clothing are considered more as cultural than religious. This is in response to the Qur'an encouragement of modest dress. All clothing which reveals contours of the body are to be avoided (Ahmed, 1999). Men might wear a boat shaped cap and/or a burgundy fez representing having made the pilgrimage to Mecca. Use of veils depends on the cultural custom. Women can be seen wearing a veil across their face, a head covering, and ankle length clothing. Muslim women wear various forms of facial veils and may chose to cover their heads, and all their hair.

Spiritual practices and Healing Traditions
Ritual prayers including prayers facing Mecca five times per day, and consider Friday prayer to be special. They participate in zakat (alms giving), fasting, pilgrimage, visiting a mosque, reading or listening to recitations of the Koran, and participating in Islamic holidays and festivals such as Ramadan. Ritual purification prior to prayer. Treating the sacred scripture with great reverence as it is the most important sacred ritual item.

Dietary Laws
Muslims follow the dietary practice of Kashrut, keeping Kosher. Certain foods are forbidden including intoxicating beverages, pork and foods prepared with pork fat, blood, and scavenger animals.

They do adhere to the separation of meat and dairy products as in the Orthodox Jewish tradition.

View of Afterlife
Death is not an end but a transition to another level of existence. They believe they are accountable for all of their earthly life decisions both positive and negative. The Qur'an speaks of the Day of Judgement and the Day of Resurrection when during the Hour when all their deeds are revealed they will travel across the narrow passage of no return to one of several destinations. Each is a varying level of heaven or hell. The highest level of heaven is called the Garden where the vision of God is obtained. Heaven is considered more a state of being than a literal place. Likewise Hell is known as the Fire and represents the refusal to acknowledge God's sovereignty.
Hell is not a permanent state and accepting God can release one from being in hell.

Abortion and Birth Control
Abortion is highly discouraged, though may be permitted only within the first 4 months of pregnancy if mother's life is at risk, or if conception was due to rape or incest. Contraception is permitted.

Sexuality
Dating is not allowed. All marriages are prearranged. The couple (of the prearranged marriage) is not allowed to be un-chaperoned. All sexual relations outside of marriage are forbidden. Homosexual behavior is forbidden.

Marriage and Divorce
Love is not a prerequisite for marriage. Marriage and children are encouraged. Dating, courtship and "romantic love" are not seen as prerequisites to marriage. Polygamy is permitted though it is illegal in the U.S. Divorce is discouraged but permitted and easier for men to obtain. Traditional families prefer arranged marriages. Prefer marriages to members of same faith, though are

not opposed to marrying outside of their tradition. In the case of interfaith marriage it is more preferable for a Muslim male to marry a non-Muslim female as it is assumed the female will convert to Islam and their children will inherit faith of the father. The male is the head of the household. God and culture ordains gender appropriate roles.

Alcohol and Illicit Drugs
Drinking alcohol and using illegal drugs are forbidden.

Medicine
Use of medication is accepted.

Suicide and Euthanasia
Suicide and direct euthanasia are forbidden, although passive forms of euthanasia may be acceptable.

View of Therapy
Most Muslims view the mental health professions with suspicion and few seek therapy. On the other hand, those who seek therapy tend to endow the mental health professional with unquestioned authority. Islam imparts personal responsibility for one's mental and physical health, and turning concerns over to God. Mental health issues are believed to be cause by lack of faith.

Religious-clinical issues
Madness is the most feared illness by Muslims (Kulwicki, 1996), Cultural and value conflicts, generation and gender conflicts, depressions and somatization, family problems, fear of mental health issues mean loss of faith, anger, depression and somatization (are intertwined in Islamic culture) with a disregard of mental issue and an acknowledgment of physical issues, enmeshment and boundary issues, co-dependency, arranged marriages, psychosis, and suicide ideation. Overly conforming since disagreeing is avoided and viewed as rude. Family might intervene on behalf of patient. Not used to making their desire known. Mixed marriages have conflicts, for example: An American woman might have

difficulty conforming to the role of the "proper" Muslim wife. The husband expects the therapist to make her conform and the wife expects the therapist to make her husband understand what is to be an American.

Assessment Recommendations
Assess what it means for the client to be a Muslim in North America. Assess client's level of acculturation, level of social and family support, and degree of religious affiliation, especially affiliation with a mosque.

Treatment Recommendations
Direct, open, and assertive communication is not appreciated or allowed in Islamic culture (Richards & Bergin, 2000). Education about religious and cultural values of Muslim clients. Family may need to be involved in treatment. Consulting with members of the Muslim community may be helpful.

Self Identified Members of Islam
1,104,000 Members
(American Religious Identity Survey, 2001)

Chapter Four - Eastern Traditions

Buddhism

What is the way of Buddha? It is the study of the self. What is the study of the self? It is to forget oneself. To forget oneself is to be enlightened by everything in the world.

-Zen Master Dogen

Siddhartha Gautama, the Buddha, was born around 536 BC. His title *Buddha* became his message. The Sanskrit root *budh* means to both wake up and to know. Buddha means the "Awakened One" or the "Enlightened One."

Siddhartha was a prince. One day his father received a prophecy about his son; he might become a great leader or a famous ascetic. Fearing for the later, his father sheltered him from the world in attempt to avoid his coming into contact with anything that might awaken his ascetic persona. But Siddhartha snuck out of the palace. In the streets of town he encountered four sights: an old man, a corpse, a sick man, and a holy man. These four sights are known in Buddhism as the Four Signs. This was the transformational occurrence that changed Siddhartha's life and established the foundation for Buddhism. He became confused, horrified, and disillusioned by the realization that old age, sickness, and death were a common fate of humankind. Before returning to the palace he saw a peaceful wandering ascetic. In the serenity of this recluse, Siddhartha sensed the only response he could make to his disillusionment.

Soon after this experience, Siddhartha left the palace, his parents, wife, and children and began his life as spiritual seeker looking for the answers to, or relief of, the inevitable suffering he witnessed. During his seeking he found himself sitting beneath a Bodhi tree vowing to sit under there until he solved the problems that besieged him. After 6 days he experienced a profound clarification of his searching; an understanding of the riddle of human existence, a freedom from crippling psychological illusions, and a vision of the path to eradicating human suffering and attaining freedom. After his enlightenment Siddhartha became a teacher.

Buddhism grew out of Hinduism. It began as a revolt against aspects of Hinduism: authority, tradition, ritual, speculation, grace, mystery, and a personal God.

Beliefs

Buddha's central teaching was the Four Noble Truths. This doctrine delineates the symptom, diagnosis, prognosis, and treatment plan for addressing human suffering (Bergin & Richards, 2000).

The First Noble Truth explains types of suffering. There is the ordinary suffering of old age, sickness, and death. The suffering caused by change. All conditioned states of mind inevitably lead to suffering. By becoming attached to what changes, humans sow the seeds of their own suffering.

The Second Noble Truth presents the causes of suffering which include desire, attachment, and craving. Suffering derives from our difficulty in acknowledging that everything in life is impermanent and transitory. Suffering arises when we resist the flow of life and cling to things, events, people, and ideas as permanent. The doctrine of impermanence also includes the notion that there is no single self, which is the subject of our changing experience (Bergin & Richards, 2000).

The Third Noble Truth is that suffering can be eradicated. It is possible to release one's self from psychological imprisonment and to reach a state of complete awakening or liberation, called *Nirvana.* In this state there is no personal desire. Without personal desire there is no grasping and suffering.

The Fourth Noble Truth describes how to experience enlightenment. It is called the Eightfold Path.

> The Eightfold Path teaches: right knowledge - awareness of where we are and where we are going, right speech - truthful, compassionate words, right thoughts and aspirations - what do we really want, right action or behavior - doing no harm to self and others, misuse of intoxicants, etc., right livelihood - working, promoting life, not harming or destroying, right effort - balanced effort to be aware, right mindfulness or concentration - seeing things clearly as they really are, and right concentration - meditative attentiveness (Smith, 1994).

Buddhism believes in reincarnation describing it in the form of a wheel of existence - a circle of birth, death and rebirth. The goal is enlightenment and to enter Nirvana.

They believe all actions (karma) have consequences, so that the person you are today will determine the person you will be in the future.

Schools of Buddhism

Theravada means the "way of the elders." Theravada teaches that the Buddha attained enlightenment on his own therefore his followers should follow his example. They believe the best way to follow Buddha is through living a monastic life. They don't put their faith in the Buddha because he has reached Nirvana.

Mahayana believes that it is possible to escape the wheel of existence by putting faith in the Buddha. Buddha is worshiped. Mahayana strive toward the becoming a "bodhisattva," a person of perfected wisdom who chooses not to cross into Nirvana until all sentient beings can cross together. Mahayana Buddhists pray to Bodhisattvas.

Vajrayana or Tantric Buddhism is practice in Tibet. This school emphasizes the use of various techniques to leave the wheel of existence. These techniques include meditation, which is central to all the schools, and the power of ritual. In contrast to other schools, the Vajrayana believe that enlightenment can be obtained in one lifetime, as opposed to taking several lifetimes on the wheel.

Zen teaches that enlightenment can be a sudden occurrence but that the student needs awakening. One way is through meditation. Meditation is central by sitting Zazen – which is something the student does and is. Zazen is sitting cross legged in contemplation, and is something one is, being lead beyond ones self as knower, to know ones self. Another way is through the use of a non-rational riddle called a Koan. Given by the teacher, the student sits and meditates on the riddle. His/her answers measure the enlightenment of the student

Most American Buddhists participate in Theravada and Mahayana, which includes Zen.

View of Deity

There is no Deity or Supreme Being. Theravada Buddhism is nontheisitc. They believe deities and gods may exist but not to help humans. Mahayana Buddhism believe that deities and gods are helping beings deserving of worship. But neither subscribe to a monotheisitic view of an absolute or reigning deity.

Spiritual practices and Healing Traditions

Meditation is central to all schools, working with one's spiritual teacher or guru, studying Buddhist teachings, daily worship and rituals, participating in holy days and festivals, and participating in rites and passages.

View of Afterlife

Buddhism believes the afterlife doesn't matter, only now, the moment, matters.

Abortion and Birth Control
Respect for life is the most important ethical principle, so abortion is viewed as unethical. Contraception is accepted.

Sexuality
One should not cause harm to others by unwholesome sexual acts, i.e. adultery. Homosexual behavior was forbidden in early Buddhism, but in contemporary American Buddhism communities, it is accepted.

Marriage and Divorce
No specific Buddhist teachings about marriage, divorce, or child rearing.

Alcohol and Illicit Drugs
Use of mind-altering substances is discouraged. Many Buddhists totally abstain from alcohol and drugs, but some American Buddhists advocate for moderate use of alcohol. Vegetarianism is often practiced but not required.

Medicine
Use of medication is accepted.

Suicide and Euthanasia
Suicide and active euthanasia are discouraged, although passive forms of euthanasia may be acceptable.

View of Therapy
A range of attitudes about therapy, including acceptance, reluctance to seek it, and active distrust of it. Debate on the merits of psychotherapy verses meditation (debate is highly praised in ancient tradition). Asian born Buddhists might not know what therapy is or could misinterpret mental illness. In their culture, the mentally ill were sheltered by their families and didn't receive outside services (Scorzelli, J. & Reinke-Scorzelli, M., 2001). American Buddhists are familiar with psychotherapy. There are a significant number of Buddhist psychotherapists.

Religious-clinical issues

Disturbed feelings, perfectionism, self-contempt, worthlessness, addictions, evading issues, submissiveness to authority, boundary issues, detachment from world and/or emotions, Crazy Wisdom – trust in a teacher is broken, pathological selflessness, seeing therapy as a failure to adhere to discipline. Asian Buddhists issues to include to the above: early emotional losses, and posttraumatic stress disorder, fear of mental illness, lack of understanding of therapy.

Assessment Recommendations

Assess the intentions shaping the client's involvement in Buddhism. Reason for conversion to Buddhism (American born). Assess level of awareness. Is the client's spiritual faith compensatory or destructive? Avoid premature judgement or dismissal of views. Avoid pathologizing.

Treatment Recommendations

Use of insight-oriented approaches, cognitive therapies, such as reality therapy and rational emotive, behavioral therapies, and Gestalt therapy are recommended. (Corey, 2001). Specific techniques that Buddhism uses for counseling include: systematic use of rewards and punishments; fear reduction by graded exposure; modeling; self-monitoring; stimulus control; overt and covert aversion; use of family members for implementing a behavior change program; and specific techniques including distraction and over exposure, from unwanted intrusive thoughts. (deSilva, .P, 1993). Supportive and encouraging meditative practices may be helpful. Consulting and working with Buddhist teachers could be helpful.

Self Identified Members of Buddhism
1,082,000 Members
(American Religious Identity Survey, 2001)

Hinduism

Hinduism recognizes a fundamental truth about humankind: People are different. From this assumption springs a religion both diverse and developmental, acknowledging the many paths that humans take to reach God, as well as, the many steps required to get there. Multiplicity and numerous stages of growth lead ultimately to oneness, to unity with *Brahman*, the undeniable, timeless, one God.

Hinduism recognizes four human temperaments: reflective and philosophical, emotional, active, empirical, or experimental. For each temperament type there is a different yoga path to God. The path is termed yoga: to place under discipline or training (to bring under the yoke). Yoga, commonly misunderstood in the West as a means of exercising the body, is more properly considered to be a spiritual path.

Hindus believe that human beings progress through four stages in their lives. Stage one: the student. Stage two, beginning with marriage, is the householder when the focus is outward on family, work or duty, and community. Stage three, begins with retirement, when the individual has lived in the external world and now turns inward. Stage four is defined in the Bhagavad Gita as "one who neither hates nor loves anything." One has achieved freedom, is unattached to the world, and has no expectations. He or she has joined the infinite.

As humans move through these stages they pursue four wants: One: the pursuit of pleasure, primarily sensual pleasure. Two: the pursuit of worldly success, such as wealth, fame, and power. Three: the desire to serve others and to be selfless in the act of helping others. Four: lifting toward *satchitananda.*

This section is devoted toward working with Hindu Indian immigrants to the U.S. Indian immigrants represent an ethnic and cultural diversity of all the countries of the Indian subcontinent, and participate in all the major religions. An assumption that the Indian is only a Hindu or Buddhist would be inaccurate.

Beliefs

Hindus believe that what humans ultimately want is to be one with God or *Brahman*. This is what they define as *satchitananda* (sat = being, chit = awareness, ananda = bliss).

The yogic paths to satchitananda are as follows: Jnana Yoga, the Path of Knowledge is designed for persons who are philosophical and intellectual and is the path to God through intuitive knowledge.

Bhakti Yoga, the Path of Love is best suited to persons whose primary way of living is through their emotions.

Karma Yoga, the Path of Work is for persons inclined to action. God may be found through the mechanics of one's daily activities.

Raja Yoga, the Path of Psychological Experimentation is designed for those scientifically and experimentally inclined. Although many regard Hinduism as purely a mystical religion, it is empirical as well.

View of Deity

Hindus believe that there is one Absolute Reality or Brahman Atman in which all deities and beings in the universe are one. There are many deities in Hinduism including many nature gods. Three main deities are Brahma the Creator, Shiva the god of destruction, and Vishnu the god of benevolence and love. The deities are communicated with, prayed to, and asked for assistance.

Spiritual practices and Healing Traditions

Meditation, yoga, religious devotions, and prayers. Rituals, festivals, and pilgrimages.

View of Afterlife

There is an unending cycle of birth, death, and rebirth. The goal, through good works and achieving good karma, is to get off the cycle of rebirth. Karma is the law of cause and effect. When the body dies, the actions of the body do not die. Instead they travel with the soul, which does not die. In its most literal form, a soul born into bitter conditions in this life is repeating the results of bad actions in past lives; conversely, a soul born into favorable circumstances is benefiting from past good deeds. The soul will reincarnate until it has transcended all feelings of pain and pleasure, and has released all fears and attachments. The development of the soul spans many lifetimes and parallels the stages of the human's life.

Abortion and Birth Control
Birth control is an acceptable practice. Abortion is accepted as a method of ending an unwanted pregnancy.

Sexuality
Sexual chastity is valued. Premarital and extramarital sex is discouraged. There is virtually no dating in Hindu society. Though in the U.S. Hindu men are allowed to date non-Hindu women, but Hindu women are not allowed to date at all. Hinduism is tolerant of homosexuality.

Marriage and Divorce
Hindu marriages are arranged by parents and unite entire families, not just the couple. Marriage and child rearing are highly valued. Divorce is strongly discouraged, though allowed under certain conditions. Divorced women are cast out. Male rules household.

Alcohol and Illicit Drugs
Alcohol use in small amounts is acceptable. Use of hard drugs is not permitted. Within some groups of use hallucinogens to enhance spiritual awareness is accepted.

Medicine
Use of medications is acceptable.

Suicide and Euthanasia
Though not considered wrong per se, suicide is not approved of as an act to escape suffering but is viewed as an act of religious merit (the ultimate austerity) for aged and venerated holy men.

Euthanasia is not permitted. Killing anyone or anything is considered wrong.

View of Therapy

General skepticism about the value of therapy. There is a cultural proscription against talking about personal and/or intimate problems with anyone other than a member of the family. And a reluctance to seek counseling because it stigmatizes the person who needs help, and their family. They feel family should take care of their own. It can be a major taboo to seek outside help. A presumable conflict between Hindu and Western counseling values. Modern Western-style counseling/psychotherapy sees development of the individual self as the essence of mental health. Even second generation Indians who have been socialized in traditional ethnic values may be reluctant to sacrifice family obligations and loyalty to advance self-centered interests in the development of the individual self (Das & Kemp, 1997).

Religious-clinical issues

Acculturation and value conflicts. Relationship issues including family issues, marital problems, dating, and marriage concerns. Gender issues including the belief that males have more value than females, role conflicts, cross-generation loyalty (mother to son, not spouse to spouse). Father choosing education, topics of study, and careers for children. Generation conflicts, appearance issues (girls and women don't wear makeup), domestic violence, and incest.

Assessment Recommendations

Assess level of acculturation and nature of the family system. Do not pathologize cultural differences. Assess where clients are in terms of development level or stage of life, student, householder, or retired. (See Beliefs)

Treatment Recommendations

A developmental therapy approach may be most natural. Cognitive-behavioral framework (Beck, 1979). Have a firm grounding in family systems theory. An intellectual approach, based on rational thinking, may be appropriate at times. Women need to be seen by a female therapist. Openness, genuineness, and honesty may be construed by clients, who value reserved and modest disclosure, as an invasion of privacy. Counseling modes that rely on introspection, reflection, and extreme client verbalization, do not meet the needs of this group (Ramisetty-Mikler, 1993). Use karma therapeutically to help clients take responsibility for their lives. Help clients explore the contradictions they feel. Learn more about the Hindu religion.

Self Identified Members of Hinduism
766,000 Members
(American Religious Identity Survey, 2001)

Sikhism

In Pakistan at approximately 1500 CE, Guru Nanak founded Sikhism. Nanak was born Hindu. Beginning as young boy, he was continually contemplated God. In his early thirties Nanak disappeared while bathing in a river. When he reappeared four days later he revealed he had a revelation from God. Instead of living life as a Hindu or Muslim (the other prominent tradition in the area) he vowed to follow only God's path. Thus he began a thirty year missionary journey to unite the Hindu and Muslim traditions. Not all Sikh's are from India. There are many Anglo-Sikh's in America.

The term Sikhism means discipleship. Therefore Sikhism is a rich mixture of both the Muslim and Hindu traditions (Edwards, 2001). (Review Hinduism and Muslim/Islam for further information).

Beliefs

To achieve union with God is the purpose of life. This is realized through loving everyone, working and praying for the highest human good, and through self-surrender and submission to God's will. Every person is valued and is viewed as part of the divine. Conquering the ego is the only way to merge the individual soul with the universal soul.

Sikhs are action oriented with a strong sense of self-reliance and follow strict disciplinary rules such as controlling the mind and body, maintaining a fearless attitude, perseverance, and constantly remembering God. Causes of forgetfulness of God include ego, hypocrisy, evil thoughts, and immoral actions (Edwards, 2001).

View of Deity

Belief in an ultimate supreme God who is beyond human explanation. God is referred to as the

Supreme Guru (spiritual teacher) who speaks to and through human gurus. Recited daily, the *Mool* Mantra, expresses Sikhs belief:

There is only one God. His name is truth.
He is the Creator. He is without fear.
He is without hate. He is beyond time (immortal).
He is beyond birth and death.
He is self-existent. He is realized by the Guru's grace.

Spiritual Practices

Life is a spiritual practice. Prayer and worship, ritual bathing, devotional singing, petitioning, meditation, prescribed moral action: actions and intent define religious status. Simplicity in clothing, material needs, food, etc. Members of *Khalsa*, initiated or true Sikhs are identifiable by the "five Ks":

Uncut hair: hair conserves energy and draws it upward, usually covered with a turban.
Comb: good order and cleanliness.
Steel Bracelet: represent hands in the service of God.
Under shorts: being dressed for immediate action.
Dagger: defense of the weak.

View of Afterlife

Salvation and union with God is the goal of the Sikh's life. Belief in reincarnation and that the soul passes through every stage of existence, which is the way the soul evolves. Karmic belief that people's deeds follow the soul. God deeds enable you to gain salvation. Practicing repentance, prayer, and love to all beings brings God's grace and neutralizes accrued karma.

Abortion

Based on Hindu and Muslim beliefs, birth control is an acceptable practice. Abortion is accepted as a method of ending an unwanted pregnancy in certain circumstances, such as rape. Within a marriage, the couple is expected to have children.

Sexuality

There is a high value placed on morality, which influences the lack of acceptance of premarital sex. Adultery is forbidden. No specific teachings on the acceptance of homosexuality.

Marriage and Divorce
Family oriented tradition, Sikhs are expected to marry and motherhood is honored. Life as the householder is viewed as the ideal. Though Sikh teachings value women as equals, women do not share equal roles as men. Divorce is frowned upon. Remarriage of a widow is acceptable.

Alcohol and Illicit Drug
Use of alcohol and drugs is forbidden as is gambling and stealing.

Medication
No formal view on the use of medication.

Suicide and Euthanasia
Suicide and direct euthanasia are forbidden, although passive forms of euthanasia may be acceptable.

No formal views on the following. However using a combination of Hindu and Muslim beliefs can provide valuable assessment information.

View of Therapy
View the mental health professions with suspicion and few seek therapy. General skepticism about the value of therapy. Sikhism imparts personal responsibility for one's mental and physical health, and turning concerns over to God. Mental health issues are believed to be cause by lack of faith.

Religious –clinical issues
Acculturation and value conflicts. Relationship issues including family issues, marital problems, dating, and marriage concerns. Perfectionism, depression, somatization, fear of mental health issues mean loss of faith, unworthiness, and anger. Gender issues including the belief that males have more value than females, role conflicts.

Assessment Recommendations

Assess what it means for the client to be a Sikh in North America. Assess client's level of acculturation, level of social and family support, and degree of religious affiliation, especially affiliation with a temple. Assess level of acculturation and nature of the family system. Do not pathologize cultural differences. Assess where clients are in terms of development level or stage of life, student, householder, or retired. (See Hindu Beliefs)

Treatment Recommendations

A developmental therapy approach may be most natural. Cognitive-behavioral framework (Beck, 1979). Have a firm grounding in family systems theory. An intellectual approach, based on rational thinking, may be appropriate at times. Use karma therapeutically to help clients take responsibility for their lives. Help clients explore the contradictions they feel. Family may need to be involved in treatment. Direct, open, and assertive communication is not appreciated. Counseling modes that rely on introspection, reflection, and extreme client verbalization, do not meet the needs of this group (Ramisetty-Mikler, 1993).

Self Identified Members of Sikhism
57,000 Members
(American Religious Identity Survey, 2001)

Baha'i Faith

The Baha'i faith was founded in the 1860's in what is modern day Iran, by Bah'u'llah, a self declared prophet who announced he was an incarnation of God. He brought a new message of faith to the world. However most of the people in the area were Muslim. As a result Baha'i shares many similarities with the religions of the book, Judaism, Christianity, most especially Islam. The prophets of all three of the above mentioned religions are held in high regard.

Beliefs
Central beliefs are: 1. The oneness of God. 2. The oneness of religion. God sent messengers such as Abraham, Moses, Krishna, Buddha, Christ, Mohammed, and Bah'u'llah to humanity to educate it in morals and in social values. 3. The oneness of humanity. All Humans come from the same source and deserve total equality. Beliefs and teachings also include the spiritual nature of human beings, prayers and religious practices to foster spiritual growth, a strong emphasis on the importance of creating unified and loving families, place a high level of importance on education, and a prescription for solving the social ills of society. The most distinctive concept of this faith is that each new age requires a new message and continuous prophecy.

View of Deity
Baha'i believes in oneness of God for the whole world. The one God is not definable, transcendent, and unknowable. God is the source of all creation. This faith believes that Eastern and Western religions are really the same thing but view God from different perspectives.

Spiritual Practices
Worship is conducted similarly to Islamic practices. Main features include individual investigation of truth through daily prayer, fasting, and pilgrimage (see Islam). There are no clergy or weekly worship service. However there is a monthly gathering call "feast"

that includes worship, consultation on community business, and social activities (Beversluis, 1995).

View of Afterlife
Baha'i's believe in life after death, but maintain that our knowledge of what it actually consists of is limited. They emphasize preparation of the soul during it's life for the rewards after death. Every person has an immortal soul that is not subject to the same deterioration as the human body. At death, the soul is free to travel to the spirit world.

Abortion
No official view on abortion.

Sexuality
All extramarital relations are forbidden. Strong disapproval of homosexuality.

Marriage and Divorce
Stable family life is emphasized in the form of monogamous marriage. Divorce is strongly discouraged but may be permitted after a "year of waiting." Children are viewed as precious.
Though women and men are considered "two wings" of humanity, there is still an inequality for women in that their belongings belong to their husbands.

Alcohol and Illicit Drug
Use of alcohol and drugs are to be avoided. (Baha'i World, 2003). Gambling and begging are forbidden.

Medication
Use of medication is acceptable.

Suicide and Euthanasia
No official view on suicide, passive euthanasia, and euthanasia

View of Therapy
Acceptance of mental health field and psychotherapy, as the Baha'i teachings stress the fundamental harmony of science and religion, but it does not identify the practice as having a direct influence on the soul (Hornby, 1988).

Religious –clinical issues
Perfection, self esteem, internal vs. external locus of control, concept of liberty and freedom, detachment, belief in immortality, social apathy or fundamentalist view, lack of self interest, separatist views, feelings of hopelessness, anger and frustration, gender issues, sexuality, materialism, and diminished parenting.

Assessment Recommendations
Assess level of involvement in the Baha'i faith.

Treatment Recommendations
Use of theories that acknowledge the spiritual essence of the person and credit the Source. Avoid "ego inflating" and focusing on personal as opposed to spiritual development. Maslow's theories are most akin to the Baha'i's belief in an external locus of control. They believe the healthy personality utilizes an intelligence that distinguishes the individual from the lower species, recognizes its own higher nature and purpose, and exercises conscience, reason, and volition. Rogers' theory is also accepted to a point. The Baha'i Faith endorses the belief that an external locus of evaluation and blind imitation of others are not indicative of a healthy personality (Bahai-library.org).

Self Identified Members of Baha'i Faith
84,000 Members
(American Religious Identity Survey, 2001)

Chapter Five - Ethnic Centered Religions and Spirituality

When reviewing the belief systems of the Asian American, the Latino/Latina, American Indian and the African American living in the U.S., it is difficult not to cross into a discussion with a more multicultural focus, than one focused on religion and spirituality. The vast populace of these four very unique groups has embraced numerous beliefs systems. Many members of these groups are practicing Christians of various denominations and have been converted either forcefully or agreeably at some earlier point of time.

The format will be slightly changed from earlier in the manual. What I will primarily highlight are the various religious and spiritual belief systems encountered in a therapeutic setting.

Asian American

To understand the Asian American it is important to know where they have come from and the corresponding cultural dictates. This group is a combination of three subgroups: Asian Americans (Japanese, Chinese, Filipinos, Asian Indians, and Koreans), Asian Pacific Islander (Hawaiians, Samoans, and Guamanians), and Southeast Asian refugees (Vietnamese, Thai, Cambodians, and Laotians) (Paniagua, 1998).

With the vast numbers of people included in these groups I will provide brief insights of what can be expected from members of the larger traditions such as Taoism, Shintoism, Confucianism, (also see Buddhism, Hinduism, Christianity.)

Taoism or Daoism

Taoism encompasses a wide variety of philosophical, religious, and magical traditions. In the 6th century BCE Lao Tzu wrote down eighty-one aphorisms that make up the book called the Tao Te Ching. After writing the book he was never seen again. The term Taoism refers to the philosophy outlined in the Tao Te Ching and to China's ancient Taoist religion (Edwards, 2001). There are many branches of Taoism, Philosophical Taoism (wise thinking) and Religious Taoism (teaching the Way).

Beliefs

The "Tao" is "the way" of the cosmos, forever fluctuating and changing. The source of everything as the underlying principle of form, substance, being, and change. It represents the driving force of universe, prevents chaos, and maintains the natural order and flow of the universe. Taoism is sometimes called the "way of water" because it teaches that we should not resist life and, like water, surrounds and flow through all things. The Tao encompasses the harmony of opposites operating as Yin and Yang. Yin and Yang represent the following opposites: negative/positive, female/male, dark/light, evil/good, earth/heaven. Tao presents instruction on the way humans can live in balance with the universal flow.

View of Deity

Religious Taoism believes in a supreme God, a supreme oneness called Tai Yi. Philosophical Taoism believes in an impersonal Tao "way" and is the only reality behind all existence. The Tao provides a moral and ethical way of acting.

View of Afterlife

Belief in transmigration of souls, reincarnation. The soul is twofold – *Hun* soul (higher soul, Yang qualities) and P'o soul (earthly soul, Yin qualities). After death the Hun soul takes a perilous journey to the underworld where it is weighed. If you are good you are light (in weight), if there are evil deeds attached to your soul you are heavy. Heavy souls are torn apart before they can continue the journey to salvation.

Shinto

Shinto is the indigenous, national religion of Japan. It can be observed more in the personal and social life's of the people than as an established theology or philosophy. The term Shinto from the Chinese words *shin tao* which means (the way of the gods). Shinto doesn't have sacred scriptures, formal doctrine, or organized priesthood.

Beliefs
At the core of Shinto beliefs are the mysterious *kami*. Each *kami* is believed to be a divine personality and to respond to sincere prayers.

View of Deity
The only deity recognized is the spiritualized human mind. Shinto holds to the way of the *kami* who are omnipresent manifestations of the sacred. *Kami* deities are of heaven and earth, of beings and places, of mountain, trees, and animals. Humanity is regarded as *"kami's* child" meaning all human life and human are sacred. *Kami* means "mysterious," "soul," "an invisible power." People can become *kami's.*

View of Afterlife
Shinto sees death as evil and has no interest in an afterlife. They are more concerned with what is happening in the here and now. Everything concerned with death is considered pollution.

Confucianism

Confucius was born around 551 BCE. His goal was to articulate a view that individuals could positively contribute to society through self-mastery and personal responsibility. Confucianism is a system of social, ethical and religious beliefs and practices associated with Confucius. Confucianism has been the main stream philosophy in China for the past two thousand years (Edwards, 2001).

Beliefs

Confucianism concentrates on human relationships and the natural human capacity for virtue with the ultimate goal of living in harmony with the will of Heaven (Renard, 2002).
The main foundational and most important of the virtues is "filial devotion."

View of Deity

Heaven is a non-personal reality and is both accessible and unknowable.
Belief in a supreme deity in Heaven as noted in this excerpt from Book of Songs, "Revere the anger of Heaven [...], Revere the changing moods of Heaven [...], Great Heaven is intelligent [...], Great Heaven is clear seeing [..]. Deities are referred to as Heaven and earth.

View of Afterlife

Death is not the end to life. The soul lives on and spiritual presence's can be felt by the living. Confucianism states that humans don't know enough about the afterlife to plan for it. Emphasis is therefore placed on the here and now.

Some Asian American Cultural Variables

Experiencing prejudice, racism, and discrimination. Emphasis on family the relationship and the extended family – family first then the individual. Defined family roles. Defined gender roles. Child's primary duty is to their parents, called "filial devotion." Parents determine the child's personal desires and ambition.

The Chinese language doesn't have words for deep feelings so there is no way to identify such emotions. They also don't have words for "privacy" and "I." This is because of they live within a communal society. The lack of these words in the language indicated their lack of relevance. Evaluating if the primary language in the home is either Chinese or Japanese may indicate that even English speaking Asians may not incorporate the concept of emotions, privacy and independence into their lives. Determining the language used in the home is vital to therapy (Renouf, 2003).

During communication they are quiet, passive, avoid offending others, avoid eye contact, are overly and sometimes inappropriately polite to avoid conflict, indirect verbal communication, long moments of silence.

Be especially aware of the high level of trauma experienced by Southeast Asian refugees/ Many come to the U.S. with a strong history of torture, killing of loved ones, missing family members, witnessed killing, sexual abuse. Evaluation for PTSD, suicidality, depression and organic brain syndrome (due to injury) (Paniagua, 1998).

Spiritual Practices

Prayer, church attendance, reading bible, worship and rituals, participation in fellowship and Bible study groups, and seeking support from pastors. Traditional practices such as acupuncture, herbal medicine, and dermabrasion (i.e. coin rubbing) may also be used simultaneously with Western medicine.

Marriage and Divorce

Women are expected to marry, be obedient, be helpers, have children, and to respect the authority of the father or husband (Paniagua, 1998). The mother-in-law is the authority of her son's wife.

Medication

Use of medication, especially herbal medicine, is expected.

View of Therapy

Asian Americans under use therapy services. They do not encourage going to someone to express their problems. Prefer to seek help from family, trusted community and spiritual leaders, traditional healers and physicians. Tend to be passive, respectful and obedient to therapist who is seen as an "authority" figure (Yamamoto, 1986).

Religious-clinical issues

Depression, shame, guilt, family issues, gender role issues, marital problems, acculturation issues, uncomfortable speaking about emotional problems, somatization. Emotional distancing, lack of emotional display or recognition, physical and verbal punishments, lack of nuturance.

Assessment Recommendations

View of mind and body as inseparable therefore they tend to express psychological issues in somatic terms. Safe to assume the issue being discussed is chronic. Avoid cultural biases in assessing functioning. Interpret assessment tools with caution in light of possible cultural biases. Formal communication, they do not expect relationship to be "personal".

Treatment Recommendations

Deal with immediate concerns and provide tangible, concrete advice, and short term intervention tools. Avoid prolonged verbal exchanges don't work well with this group. Be directive, but use restraint in gathering information. Treat somatic disorders as real. Avoid direct confrontations and undue emphasis on emotions. Use the support network of family, friends, church, and community to help clients. Spiritual interventions may be helpful. Consulting with religious leaders may be helpful.

Self Identified Members of Taoism
40,000 Members
Self Identified Members of Shintoism
30,000 Members approximate

Self Identified Members of Confucianism
1,000,000 Members approximate
(American Religious Identity Survey, 2001)

Self Identified Asian Americans
10,000,000 Members
(Population Reference Bureau, 2003)

African American

In 1972 Wade Nobles introduced Black psychology in the form of specific philosophical values, customs, attitudes and behaviors shared by many African Americans. The inclusion of religion and spirituality was and still is prominently featured as being significant to the lives and therapeutic well being of this population (Nobles, 1972). Religion is integrated into the African American's life just as naturally as breathing. According to J. Mbiti traditional African culture doesn't separate spirituality from one's personal identity (Mbiti, 1991). The traditional cultural mores were passed on from generation to generation and are alive and well in contemporary culture.

When Africans were taken from their homeland and transported to America to be slaves attempts were made to wipe out their cultural identity. Instead, their spiritual identity became a bastion of relief, solace, and survival. They gathered in secret, and often veiled gatherings

(covert communication of the sacred through music and dance) and found strength and unity in the presence of God. Eventually (1600's) some slaves adopted Christian forms of worship to their native spirituality and began organizing their own worship services thus beginning the first African American Churches.

Islam was originally brought to the U.S. by slaves in the seventeenth century. As many as 20% of the slaves were Muslim (Wormser, 1994). We now see African American embracing a rich diversity of denominations including Jehovah Witness, Seventh Day Adventist, Roman Catholic, Methodist, Pentecostal, Baptist, Presbyterian, Lutheran, and Episcopalian Christianity, and Islam.

Much of what is covered regarding individual denominations can be found in earlier chapters in this manual. For specifics about the African American view, read on.

Some African American Cultural Variables

Racial liberation is in the forefront of many aspects of ministry including worship services, social services, and political action. Identity includes internalized oppression. Many have not faired well in the criminal justice system and are suspicious of evaluation tools and legally reporting issues that could tear the family apart. References to God and prayer are ingrained within the African American culture. Two important terms to be familiar with are "church home" and "church family" (Smith, 1985). "Church home" is the church regular attended by the family, which often include driving great distances to go "home". "Church family" is the family of church members, extended family views of "brothers and sisters" all in the church community including the minister and his family (Boyd-Franklin, 1989).

Beliefs

For most is the belief that the nature of God and His created world is trusting and benevolent. God is present anywhere, anytime, and can be spoken with always (Mitchell & Mitchell, 1989).

The psyche and spirit are seen as one (Nobles, 1980: Mbiti, 1970). Beliefs are communal so spiritual and social experiences are shared. Community is extremely important and in so being many churches have developed resources for the basic needs of their members. Many of the beliefs are practiced from a fundamentalist perspective. (See Fundamentalism).

View of Deity

Belief in the Trinitarian deity of God the Father, Jesus Christ the Son, and the Holy Spirit. Jesus is called upon for liberation, reconciliation, healing and guidance. Faith is alive.

Spiritual practices and Healing Traditions

One acts out religious meaningfulness and consciousness at anytime and in any place (Mbiti, 1991). Community fellowships, worship including sermons, prayer, scriptural readings, music, dancing, clapping, shouting, rituals such as baptism, communion, laying on of hands, symbolic imagery, and anointing with oil, and seeking spiritual direction from pastors. Many aspects of worship can provide a cathartic experience.

View of Afterlife
Viewed as home going rituals, funerals are celebrations for having endured life on earth and being rewarded with eternal life in heaven.

Abortion
Varying views depending on denomination participation.

Sexuality
Strong emphasis placed on male to female relationships and the nuclear family. Sexuality, and sexual abuse and incest are not talked about openly. For particular views on premarital sex refer to the particular denomination. Varying views on homosexuality depending on the conservative or liberal nature of the church.

Marriage and Divorce
Many still hold to the literal Biblical mandate of man as head of household (Bergins & Richards, 2000).

Alcohol and Illicit Drug
Varying views on the use of alcohol though many admonish the use of both alcohol and drugs.

Medication
Some may be reluctant to take medication as it reflects doubt in God's ability to heal. Also many African Americans were involuntary clinical treatment trials (e.g. Tuskeegee syphilis experiment) and have negative views of medication (Bergin & Richards, 2000).

Suicide and Euthanasia
Varying views depending on denomination participation.

View of Therapy
Perceptions of therapy vary across denominations. In past, African American churches have been suspicious of counseling, but in recent years have become more open to it. May be very cautious about using psychotropic medications.

Religious-clinical issues
Relationship issues, depression, depression seen as possession, feelings of hopelessness and worthlessness, grief, racial identity development, discouragement to reveal emotional pain, overeating, sexual abuse and incest, and potential for negative responses to addictions, sexual abuse and incest, and homosexuality.

Assessment Recommendations
Clinical interviews are recommended for assessing client's spirituality because of lack of "norm" assessment instruments for this population. Assess client's church history, relationship with God, and spiritual experiences and practices. Assess the client's relationship with God, by finding out which God is in their lives, how they experience and communicate with God apart from the church, and in what ways do they gain strength from God.

Treatment Recommendations
Empathic understanding is essential. Biblical and personal narratives, and supportive cognitive-behavioral techniques, may be helpful. Directive approach is advised as this population is advised on life regularly by their pastor. History taking may be perceived as intrusive if done prematurely. Testing may be viewed with suspicion. An active awareness of the part of the therapist regarding the effects of racism can be seen as supportive (Renouf, 2003).

Self Identified African Americans
36,419,434 Members
(Population Reference Bureau, 2003)

Latino/Latina

No single tradition represents the entire Latino culture. They range from Indigenous to Roman Catholic, encompass Christian denominations, and Judaism. The terms Latino/Latina refer to people born to Latin American ancestry. Latinos don't belong to a single race group but may be multiracial. The diversity of the people is also reflected in their spiritual belief systems.

Some Latino/Latina Cultural Variables

Latinos health is a complex mixture of physical, psychological, social and spiritual factors.

Two views on the causes and treatment of mental and physical issues – traditional and folk illnesses or supernatural, magic, or bewitchment caused illness. Though unrelated to religious beliefs folk illnesses can become issues in the therapeutic relationship. They include: the evil eye (*mal de ojo*), fright (*susto or espanto*), indigestion (*empacho*), nerves (*nervios*) and nervous attacks (*ataques de nervios*). Underlying folk illnesses are the beleifs in the power of strong emotions to influence bodily health (Walsh, 1999). Folk healers are called *Curanderos* though *brujas* and *Yerberos* (herbalists) may also be employed. Because the following ailments are found to be applicable to several traditions they are included here for general knowledge.

Evil Eye: social relations contain inherent dangers to the well being of the individual and that someone is exerting overpowering influence on another. Symptoms of evil eye include severe headache, uncontrollable weeping, fretfulness, insomnia and fever.

Fright: can affect anyone at any age. Symptoms include restlessness, listlessness, diarrhea, vomiting, weight loss, or lack of motivation (Tseng & McDermott, 1981).

Indigestion: caused by complex social and physiological factors.

Nerves: state of distress. Also described as "brain aches." Symptoms include headaches, sleep difficulties, trembling, tingling, dizziness, simple anxiety or nervousness.

Attack of nerves: Sense of being out of control. Symptoms include dissociative experiences, hyperkinesis, seizure like activity, fainting mutism, hyperventilation, crying spells, shouting. The victim may experience amnesia surrounding the attack (Walsh, 1999).

Mal puesto or brujeria (bewitchment) are the causes of chronic, prolonged and unexplained ailments such as social disruption, unrequited love, quarrels and breakups, conflicts within a family, infertility, some forms of mental illnesses including schizophrenia and insanity.

There are black and white witches (*brujo or bruja*). Black magicians cause harm and white cure. Contemporary witches are consulted for a wide variety of problems.

Beliefs and View of Deity

Espiritismo or spiritualism refers to an invisible world of good and evil spirits who can attach themselves to humans beings and influence their behavior (Garcia-Preto, 1996). Distress is often seen as originating from supernatural sources. Use of mediums to contact spirits is widely accepted.

Santeria or "The religion" worships a High God who created the universe. God is not involved in human affairs, but has left his saints on earth. The saints or spirits influence human behavior. Santeria deities are a combination Yoruban (African) and Catholic saints. Homage is paid to the spirits and saints. *Santeros* (priests or priestesses) function as healers, diviners, and ritual directors by functioning in both the material and the spiritual world. Santeria is primarily practiced by Cubans and Puerto Ricans.

A combination of Santeria and spiritualism gave birth to the widely practiced belief system called Spiritism. Within Spiritism god rules a universe in which all beings are ranked in order of spiritual purity thus creating a hierarchy of spiritual and human beings. It is believed that each person attracts to them like energy of spirits. Many seek guidance from the spirits around them.

In Yoruba there is also a main God who "divinized ancestors" who have control over forces of nature.

Many Latino/Latina people are Christians and uphold a Trinitarian belief system and view of a deity. Therefore refer to the appropriate applicable denomination.

Spiritual practices and Healing Traditions
Community support, seeking direction from spiritual leaders, rituals, prayer, masses, ceremonies, divination, blessings, sacrifices, and consultation with the spirit world.

View of Afterlife, Abortion, , Alcohol and Illicit Drug, Medication, Suicide and euthanasia
No formal or universal view on these issues is available. Assess the individual or family beleifs is recommended.

Sexuality
Sex roles are clearly delineated with the father as the head of the household. Sexual behavior of females is severely restricted while freedom is given to males. As head of household males are expected to be strong, dominant, and the provider for the family (machismo), while women are expected to nurturant, submissive to the male and self-sacrificing (marianismo) (Sue & Sue, 2003). In Mexican cultures women are expected to a baby before she is 20 years of age to prove her worth as a female.

Marriage and Divorce
Marriage is expected and divorce is frowned upon.

Religious-clinical issues
Acculturation and value conflicts, racial-ethnic identity issues, sexuality, anger and stress, marriage and family issues, depressions, occupational stress, and gender role issues. *"Fatalismo"* is a cognitive orientation (Comas-Diaz, 1989). It is a fatalistic outlook, which increases psychological distress and created by limited opportunities to get ahead and change life circumstances. *Controlarse* or control is also a cognitive and behavioral mechanism for mastering the challenges of life by controlling one's moods and emotions, particularly anger, anxiety and depression (Walsh, 1999).

Mental psychological and emotional problems and solutions are seen as resulting from luck, fate, or powers beyond the control of the individual. They are sometimes seen as God's test, or God's will (Walsh, 1999). Within Spiritism, fugue states, disassociation, seizures and "attack of nerves" are attributed to spirits.

Assessment Recommendations

Determine the level of involvement in, and which belief system the Latino follows. Do not assume pathology when clients are mediums or seek consultation from them. Inclusion of spirits is common for some so caution is advised when assuming pathology Use clinical interview to assess client's spiritual beliefs. No objective measures are available for this group, as they don't cover the range of beliefs.

Treatment Recommendations

Individualistic intervention approaches are less congruent with Latino worldview than group/family included intervention techniques. Consultation with spiritual leaders and practitioners may be helpful. Therapy in combination with body work may help increase effectiveness (Renouf, 2003).

Self Identified Latino/Latina Americans
35,305,818 Members
(Population Reference Bureau, 2003)

Native American

To understand the observant Native American, one must understand that the Native American's life is a total immersion in the Sacred. The Sacred knowledge, ways, and practice (participation) encompass the notion of what can be considered to be the religion and spirituality of the Native American. The Native American acknowledges no difference between living and their expression of spirituality.

The religion and spiritually of the Native American is a very complex, as all the different tribes, approximately 2 million people representing 542 tribal groups and 150 languages (U.S. Bureau of Census, 1991), have religion and spirituality as a cultural value and belief. Each individual tribal expression of religion and spirituality is unique, which adds to the difficulty in addressing the topic. Native Americans have a special concern with what and how information about their religion and spirituality is disseminated. Even in aboriginal times, the Sacred was protected and remained secret.

Some Native American Cultural Variables

From aboriginal times, religion and spirituality have played a powerful role in the life and survival of the Native American. Many aspects of their lives have been strongly challenged. Historically, these challenges include attempts to eliminate, at worst, or assimilate, at best, the Native Peoples. These attempts include:

1. Deliberate extermination
2. relocating them from their native land
3. use boarding schools to increase assimilation both societal and religiously
4. destruction of the valued aspects of the peoples' culture
5. destruction and outlawing the Native Americans' religion, spirituality, and language

These historical events continue to have an impact on their present-day lives and culture, contributing to their problems, conflicts, and stress of coexisting with the culture that destroyed their way of life.

Most Native Americans haven't abandoned the values, beliefs, and practices of their cultural heritage. Religion and spirituality are recognized extensively among those who maintain their tribal traditions, which have endured the test of time with each passing generation.

Native Americans emphasize a nonverbal communication style. Moderation in speech and avoidance of direct eye contact indicates nonverbal communicators of respect by the listener, especially respected elders or authority figures. Native Americans usually speak softly (if at all) and take ample time to reflect before responding. Therefore, many who are acting culturally appropriate may be labeled as "slow," "passive," "withdrawn," "uncooperative, " "lazy," or "unassertive" by members of mainstream society.

Beliefs
Sacred knowledge, ways, and practices generate the necessary rituals, ceremonies, and prayers for each tribe to maintain its unique expression. Tribal traditions use religious and spiritual events to express the invisible (i.e. the mystical and experiences beyond the ordinary) aspects of the sacred with manifestations that are visible (i.e. rituals expressed through dance). The Native American life experience is characterized with a distinct view of the world and a unique perception of reality, in which everyday life is integrated into religion as an expression of spirituality (Beck & Walters, 1977).

Each tribe is distinct and diverse, and adds to the rich tapestry of the various unique tribes that make up the Native American cultural heritage. Yet, with all the diversity of the tribal groups across the United States, respect prevails among the different tribes.

The basis for this respect includes a number of factors common to all the tribes: their common bond as Native Americans, their cultural heritage, similarities in history and life experiences, and the critical factor of religion and spirituality (Beck & Walters, 1977). Although the different tribes maintain their respective traditional values, beliefs, and practices, there are a number of shared views that most tribes have in common:

1. A belief or knowledge about the unseen powers, reference is to deities and spirits, mysteries, and great powers.
2. Knowledge that all things in the universe are dependent on each other. The notion of balance and harmony.
3. Personal worship creates the bond among the individual, tribal members, and the great powers; worship is a personal commitment to the source of life
4. The responsibility of persons knowledgeable in the Sacred to teach and guide their tribe in the Native American way of life.
5. For most tribes, a Shaman or Medicine person is responsible for specialized secret Sacred knowledge. Oral tradition is used by the shaman to pass Sacred knowledge, ways, and practices from generation to generation.

View of Deity

In the Native American tradition the circle is a symbol of power, relation, peace, and unity. This is where the Great Mystery or the Divine reveals itself. It serves as a reminder of the sacred relationship all people share with all living beings in this world. It is a symbol of the responsibility as a helper and contributor to the flow of the Circle of Life, better known as the Medicine Wheel, by living in harmony and balance with all our relations (Garret & Carroll, 2000). To Native Americans the statement, "All our Relations" means all the two legged – people, all the four legged – animals, all the winged – birds, all that swims, crawls, the plant people, rock people, sun, moon, minerals, wind, water, fire, thunder, rain, etc. All creation animate or inanimate in Western terms, is included. To the Native American everything has energy making everything alive and to be honored as Sacred. They also believe that all life is interdependent. This belief is reflected in Chief Seattle's words that, " all things are connected like the blood which unites one family (Archuletta, lecture, 09/20/01). The Great Mystery reveals itself as the powers of the four directions, and these four powers provide the organizing principle for everything that exists in the world. To gain self-awareness and enlightenment, one has to be in harmony with the powers of the four directions and the source of life. The medicine wheel symbolized by a cross within a circle provides a tool for achieving this balance and harmony.

Many Native Americans are practicing Christians and should be assessed with their denomination and culture in mind.

Spiritual practices and Healing Traditions

Rituals such as vision quests, prayers, healing ceremonies, songs and dances, experiencing sacred moments such as dreams and visions, seeking to live in harmony and balance with nature, seeking knowledge and wisdom from the shaman or medicine man. For the Native American people, their religious and spiritual experiences are daily life events that surround them all the time. They may be in personal worship from the time they rise in the morning until they go to sleep at night. They commemorate every aspect of life. Personal worship helps keep the Native American in contact with themselves, family, tribe, and all other important religious and spiritual needs (Lomawaima, Lecture, 08/28/01).

View of Afterlife, Abortion, Sexuality, Marriage and Divorce, Alcohol and Illicit Drug, Medication, Suicide and Euthanasia

No formal or universal view on these issues. Assess views on these issues with the individual when appropriate. Some tribes such as the Navajo, have a taboo regarding death. They do not enter a place where a death has occurred or touch any material items associated with dead. Assess for tribal views on death. Often considered a matriarchal cultural though the male is head of the household. As a communal society, clan relations within tribal community are very important.

View of Therapy

Native Americans will seek help from the Shaman or medicine man first. Most are willing to seek medical assistance, but many will not seek help for mental health problems unless the provider has built a trusting relationship by demonstrating cultural competence over time. In many cases problems exist because their attitudes toward mental health services, such as lack of awareness of the services offered, fear and mistrust, and a negative attitude toward the mental health profession.

Religious-clinical issues
Alcoholism and drug abuse, acculturation conflicts, ethnic identity, depression, suicide, social discord, family and parent – child problems, low self esteem, and unemployment and poverty, murder, accidental death and injury, assault, theft, unemployment and divorce (Price, 1975).
Also included are developmental disabilities, anxiety, alienation, medical issues such as high blood pressure, kidney failure, and diabetes. Native American adolescents have lives filled with stressors and are seen to be extremely susceptible to high stress levels related to problems and developmental task of identity formation. Also high rates of children running away, teen pregnancy, and dropping out of school. They feel particularly caught between two cultures.

Assessment Recommendations
Cultural competence is needed to conduct a valid assessment. Assess level of acculturation, ethnic identity, and spiritually in the context of the Native American's life experience. Be cautious not to impose cultural biases in assessing functioning and pathology. What is important is to recognize that Native Americans have mental health problems, which are reasons for seeking mental health services. Depression is the most frequently reported mood disorder presented (U.S. Department of Health and Human Services, 1995). The causes for depression are related to poverty, lack of employment, racial discrimination, geographical isolation, inadequate educational opportunities, health concerns such as high blood pressure, kidney failure, poor nutrition, and diabetes, psychological and cultural identity issues, and historical issues. The presence of mental illness, dysfunction, or self-destructive

behaviors impacts approximately 480,000 or 21% of the total Native American population (U.S. Department of Health and Human Services, 1990). Direct confrontation is avoided because it disrupts the harmony and balance that are essential to being. Many Native Americans will experience discomfort with what is perceived as intrusive questioning or the demand for disclosure (Garrett, 1994). Humor is a wonderful tool to use with this population. Native Americans love to laugh and display a very dry sense of humor.

Other recommendations include: asking permission whenever possible and giving thanks, never interrupt, allow sufficient time for completion and contemplation of thoughts, be patient, use silence whenever it seems appropriate, use descriptive statements rather than questioning, model self-disclosure through anecdotes or short stories, and make use of metaphors and imagery when appropriate (Garrett, 1994).

Treatment Recommendations

Cultural competence is essential to establishing a meaningful relationship basic to clinically interacting with the Native American. It's important to establish a trusting, person-to-person relationship. Be sensitive to cultural and spiritual beliefs and values. Do not violate the sacred. One way to incorporate spirituality is the use of the Medicine Wheel. Use interventions that respect client's worldview and belief in the importance or relationships with the land, wildlife, water, community, etc. consult with a traditional healer. Native Americans best respond to treatment methods that are ethnic specific and recognize their history of coercion and current symptoms. Develop non-verbal communication skills, learn to recognize and reflect non-verbal behaviors, and not to rely exclusively on individual counseling techniques, as family therapy techniques work well (Beck, 1979). Regarding substance abuse, behavior change is the goal. Often cognitive, behavioral, and insight-oriented therapies are the theoretical underpinnings of treatment for substance dependence. Often they have become distanced from their spiritual roots. Therefore encouraging a return to their innate spiritual nature and traditions is often the first step in healing their emotional issues.

Self Identified Native Americans
2,000,000 Members
Representing 542 tribal groups and 150 languages
(U.S. Bureau of Census, 1991)

Chapter Six - Pagan and Occult Practices – Shamanism, Wicca, Druidry

The number of adherents to Pagan Traditions has grown rapidly over the past several decades and continues to grow. The fastest growing religion (in terms of percentage) is Wicca -- a Neo-pagan religion that is sometimes referred to as Witchcraft. Numbers of adherents went from 8,000 in 1990 to 134,000 in 2001. Wiccan adherents are doubling in number about every 18 months. (American Religious Identification Survey, 2002). Numbers of new adherents to Druidry and Shamanism are just as impressive.

Many have converted to these traditions in search of "religion" where both the physical and spiritual are celebrated and where the adherent is personally involved in the honoring celebration. Each of these traditions has their roots planted in antiquity surviving millennia of ridicule, torture, and death. Yet they these traditions survived and thrive in contemporary society.

These three traditions have many similarities the first being that they are not "organized" in the same way as other formal religions. There is no single leader, authority, teacher or prophet. No sacred texts or literature, no ruling body or collaborative system in charge of the various practicing groups. This was done on purpose so each individual and/or group functions as a dynamic, accessible, and unique system unto itself thus enabling each person to experience the divine in their own way. Many practitioners of these traditions are, as Wiccan's are defined, "Solitary practitioners."

Within the membership of these traditions can be found a vast variety of views on issues such as abortion, war, sexuality, suicide, etc. Since there is no way to acquire an "official view" on any issue, they will not be addressed in this manual.

It is safe to say that therapy is not an unusual concept to this group as the majority have lived in mainstream society longer than they have participated in one of these traditions. The growth of these traditions in the U.S. is only approximately 20-30 years old, which is a liberal estimate, with many "first generation" participants. Only now are we seeing second generation Wiccan's born to Wiccan parents and living their tradition from birth.

What I will provide is the essential "need to know" information about each tradition so the therapist has an understanding of the adherents basic beliefs and worldview. The following definitions are to assist the reader in differentiating terms used in relation to these groups:

Animism – A view that everything, animals, plants, rocks, wind, fire, air, etc. has a spirit/soul. Animism is the foundation of Shamanism.

Earth Centered Spirituality – The honoring of the interconnectedness of life on the planet. Earth is viewed as feminine: Mother or Gaia, or sometimes as the gender neutral Earth Spirit. Other names for this tradition include Earth Religion or Gaian Religion.

Goddess Spirituality – Revering the Great Goddess in one or more of her many forms, as well as, honoring nature. Usually polytheistic and sometimes multicultural in practice. Usually incorporates feminine perspectives

(Beversluis, 1995).

Heathen – Originally meant one who dwelled on the heath (country flatlands), but later became associated with an unbeliever of mainstream religion. Another name for Pagan.

Nature Religions – Religions that include honoring the Divine as immanent in Nature. Usually polytheistic and animistic and considered the traditional ways of native peoples.

New Age – The term is used for various movements such as the green movement, alternative healing, astrology, occultism, Wicca, Druidry, Shamanism, and many Eastern traditions. The belief is that the planet and all on it have entered a new age of spiritual evolution with an emphasis on healing the body, mind and spirit, to develop a personal experience of the sacred, and to realize their inner potential.

Neo-pagan – Contemporary Pagan

Occult – "hidden." Occult beliefs envelope a host of ancient traditions including the practices of the Celts, Egyptians, witchcraft, Astrology, and many of the same practices found in new age belief.

Pagan – Originally referred to a "country dweller" or one who dwelled on the heath. Now it is most familiarly used to refer to a practitioner of contemporary or ancient Nature religion.

Polytheism – Honoring divinity in two or more forms as in many gods, and/or multiple aspects within one deity such as masculine and feminine in one god essence. Nature spirits are also polytheistic.

Shamanism

Shamanism represents the most widespread and ancient methodological system of mind-body healing known to humanity. Archeological and ethnological evidence suggests that shamanic methods are at least twenty to thirty thousand years old (Harner, 1980). Therefore it is the oldest system of healing in the world. Though Shamanism is prevalent in tribal cultures it can be found all over the world. The ancestors of tribal cultures used shamanic healing to maintain health, strength, to cope with serious illness, and to deal with the threat and trauma and of death.

Varying forms of Shamanism include Traditional which is practiced by indigenous tribes, and Multicultural, which are contemporary forms that integrate old and new ways of spirit travel from several cultures.

Beliefs
A Shaman is an adept who serves as a healer and spirit world communicator for others. The
Shaman learns to function in two realities, the ordinary and the non-ordinary. The non-ordinary is the shamanic altered stated of consciousness, which varies from light trance to deep coma. The Shaman enters into trance then travels to the spirit or lower world, usually through a hole or opening in the earth. It is in the lower world and in the trance state that enables the shaman to see and do things within the non-ordinary state, such as see into the future, see illness, find lost souls, learn cures for disease, obtain knowledge, healing, visions, and understanding. Shamans have long believed that their powers were the powers of the animals, of the sun, and of the basic energy of the universe (Harner, 1980). Shamans are believed to have the ability to shape shift while in trance. The shamans power animal is considered the Shamans alter ego. It provides him/her the ability and power to transform (shape shift) from human form into animal form, usually that of their power animal, and back again.

View of Deity
This is an animistic tradition believing that everything has a soul/spirit including plants, animals, rocks, the wind, sun, air, etc. Each Shaman has a guardian spirit in the form of an animal, fish, bird, reptile, and sometimes human. The guardian protects him/her from illness and from negative forces.

Spiritual Practices
Healing is the most important goal of Shamanism. To heal the shaman needs to enter the trance state. To enter the trance state the following may be used individually or together: singing, chanting, drumming, rattling, dancing, ceremonial ritual, and ingesting hallucinogens (Drury, 1996).

View of Afterlife
Shamanism involves many out-of body experiences, and death and dismemberment during the trance state. Fear of death may not be as prevalent with this group - check with each individual. Belief in reincarnation.

Religious –clinical issues
Any variety of issues could present from this group especially chronic issues due to belief in self healing *over* assisted healing, abuse of shamanic power – power over others, sexual abuse, hallucinations, and substance abuse. Intense self –examination whether individual is or isn't ready, fear, guilt. The initiation into shamanism is similar to the Native American vision quest – a vigil of one to several days in the wilderness, with no sleep, shelter, fire, or food. Though an initiation ceremony can be performed, some Shamans are spontaneously initiated. This type of initiation might not be expected, planned, or wanted. It could last for days up to years. Drury refers to the Shaman's journey as a "control act of mental dissociation" (Drury, 1996). If it is not a planned experience, a number of responses to a journey could occur including fear and confusion.

Assessment Recommendations

Assess for level of involvement in shamanic practices, whether or not they are a shamanic practitioner (someone learning to and working with shamanic practices for self-development or for others), how often they "travel" to the lower world, and the outcomes of the travel. Assess for use of hallucinogens (not all use mind altering substances).

Treatment Recommendations

Variety of modalities can be used with this group. Base treatment on you assessments.

Wiccan Shamanism

Wiccan Shamanism combines witchcraft and shamanism with an interfaith and multicultural focus. It blends Wicca, transpersonal psychology, and cross-cultural shamanistic traditions, while drawing on both old and new practices.

Belief
The Wiccan Rede of harming none is combined with the shamanic practice of discovering one's personal relationship with the spirits of nature and finding one's power animals and plants for the purpose healing.

Spiritual Practices
Healing is the most important facet of Wiccan Shamanism. Healing can take place by an individual or in a healing circle. Ceremonies are comprised of singing, chanting, drumming, rattling, ecstatic dancing, and meditation. Wiccan Shamanism does not participate in the use of illegal substances. Ceremonial tools include drums, rattles, feathers, herbs, crystals, stones, tree bark and other natural objects. Wiccan Shamanism also includes training in dream craft, herbology and positive magic.

There are no recorded numbers of adherents or practitioners of Shamanism

Wicca

Wicca or Wicca Spirituality is a contemporary Nature Religion rooted in the folk traditions of old Europe. It is also known as the Old Religion, the Craft, Wicce, Ways of the Wise, Neo-pagan, Witchcraft, and Benevolent Witchcraft. Many Wiccans prefer the term wicca rather than witch or witchcraft due to the negative stereotypes attached to the words.

Wicca is an organized, non-dogmatic, religion with its own beliefs, tenets, laws, ethics, holy days and rituals. The most important of these being the Wiccan Rede which acknowledges the right of all people to choose their own paths as long as their choices don't injure or harm themselves or others (see below).

Varying groups of practitioners include the Celtic, Norse, Welsh, Greek, Italian, and Lithuanian, to name a few. Also there are those who follow a particular teaching or teacher such as Gardnerians who follow the teachings of Gerald Gardner, and those who follow the path of a one deity, such as the Dianic group who hold the goddess Diana as the Divine figurehead.

Beliefs

All people have the capacity and the responsibility to experience the sacred mystery that gives life true meaning. This insight is achieved through living in harmony with the Earth (Curott, 1995). Though there are numerous variations on the expression of Wicca some basic concepts are shared by all practitioners. They are:

The Goddess and God are revered.

Human souls enjoy a series of incarnations in human form.

Power can be sent to non-physical form to affect the world in positive ways.

What is done will be returned to the doer.

The Earth is our home, our Goddess. Wiccans aren't evangelical. Wicca accepts that every religion is correct to its adherents. Wicca accepts members from both sexes, from every race, national origin, and, usually, every sexual preference.

Wicca is a religion, not a political organization.

Wicca doesn't charge for private lessons or for initiation (Cunningham, 1997).

<u>View of Deity</u>

The divine is experienced in all that is done and in all that is, including prayer, ritual, gardening, and taking out the trash. It can be found in the air, the water, the food, and each other. It is up to the individual as to whether they classify the divine as feminine, as a multiplicity or as a dyad of feminine and masculine together. The Goddess seen as both transcendent and immanent is an essential aspect of Wiccan worship. She may be worshiped as the nameless single Goddess or in one of many of her forms. Wiccans hold extreme reverence for the Earth and are very ecologically minded.

<u>Spiritual Practices</u>

Wiccan spiritual practices most often referred to as magic are actually ancient techniques for changing consciousness at will in order to develop one's gifts, and to live a full, joyous and spiritual life, to better perceive and participant in Divine reality (Curott, 1995).

Practical aspects include healing techniques, divination, purification, blessings, raising energy, prayer, meditation, ritual, drumming, singing and chanting, dancing, journeying, and trance states. "Casting a spell" is a ritual of drawing one's own inner Divine energy outward to manifest in the world through harmonious interaction with the external Divine presence. Wicca is attuned to the natural rhythm of nature with rituals and celebrations coinciding with the lunar cycle. They celebrate the Equinoxes, solstices, as well as seasonal festivals.

<u>View of Afterlife</u>

Many hold the belief of the cycle of birth, death and rebirth and a strong belief in reincarnation.

Religious –clinical issues

Persecutory beliefs, prejudice or paranoia, being misunderstood and concealing belief out of fear, depression.

Assessment Recommendations

Assess level of involvement in this tradition. Standard assessment tools are appropriate for this group.

Treatment Recommendations

Variety of modalities can be used with this group. Base treatment on you assessments.

Self Identified Wicca and Pagans
750,000 Members
(American Religious Identity Survey, 2001)

Druidry

Druidry is a very obscure tradition with little accurate information to be found but with enough speculation, tall tales, and fantasy to go around for centuries. Even contemporary writings are based more on theory than fact. There are no records of their origins nor is it known with any certainty when they were first active (Matthews, 1999). Druidry was totally an oral tradition. Those who were more interested in their destruction (i.e. the Romans) than preserving accurate historical accounts wrote many accounts of Druids with a decidedly slanted point of view. Over the centuries numerous fantastical stories have been written about the Druids. Therefore most of what is inferred about them comes from what is *not* said in the history books (Matthews, 1999).

But even with all this ambiguity groups of individuals gather together to recreate, as best, or intuitively, as they know how, ancient rites long forgotten. Philip Carr-Gomm, Chief of the order of Bards, Ovates and Druids suggests that Druidry exists in the spiritual, archetypal world and that each generation must attempt to connect with and express this ideal, potential or archetype as best as it can. He also suggests that Druidry should be available within all religions. Many contemporary Druids concentrate on learning as much as they can about actual ancient rites in order to rebuild a druidic tradition. Druidry is more a philosophy that religion.

The origin of the word Druid may come from the Celtic word-roots *durwid* – dur meaning 'oak' and *wid* meaning 'knowledge or to know'. The classical sources do not refer to Druids as "only" priests or consider Druidry as a religion, as in the more contemporary views.

Within ancient Druidry there were three specialties: Bards were the keepers of tradition and the memory of the tribe. Ovates worked with the processes of death and regeneration, were healers, and specialized in divination, spirit communication and prophesizing. The Druids and Druidesses were the professional class in Celtic society. They were doctors, lawyers, teachers, psychologists, historians, prophets, astronomers, and political advisors. Druids led all public rituals.

Many contemporary Druids may base their practices on ancient Celtic traditions called Celtic Paganism, so they are also known as Celtic Pagans, Neo-pagan Druids, Celtic Reconstructionists, Christian Druids, Pagan Druids, and Bards.

Beliefs

Druidry can be practiced in a solitary manner or in a group. Dogma is abhorred. As in ancient times, there is an emphasis on education. An ancient Druid length of study is approximately twenty years.

While no two Druids will believe exactly the same way or worship the same gods, there are some commonalties:

They can monotheistic or polytheistic. Some druids are also practicing Christians. A minority follows a racist or nationalistic agenda. They are usually animists, believing that everything in nature possesses a soul or spirit. Druidry is a solar tradition with the sun position in the sky as the primary source of cyclical celebrations. They practice magic. Most celebrate the solstices and equinoxes. They revere nature and are actively involved in sustaining a balanced ecology. They honor their ancestor (Religious Movements, 2003).

View of Deity

Celts were organized into tribes. As a result over 374 Celtic local deities have been recorded into archeological evidence. There is also evidence of a main pantheon of gods and goddesses that total to approximately three dozen. Most of the deities are worshiped as a triune or triple aspect. Druids often refer to the divine as the fire in the head or the divine spark.

Spiritual Practices
Baptism (similar to those found in Buddhism, Christianity, Islam), rituals, divinations, fire-festivals on the first of each of four months, similar to seasonal festivals, magical rites,

View of Afterlife
Druids believe the soul is immortal and continues to live new lives in another human body. The God Bile (also known as Bel, Belenus) transports the dead to the otherworld (another plane of existence). Life continues there in human form, as it did here before death. When someone dies in the Otherworld they are reborn on this plane.

Religious –clinical issues
Persecutory beliefs, prejudice or paranoia, being misunderstood and concealing belief out of fear, depression

Assessment Recommendations
Assess level of involvement in this tradition. Standard assessment tools are appropriate for this group.

Treatment Recommendations
Variety of modalities can be used with this group. Base treatment on you assessments.

There are no recorded numbers of adherents or practitioners of Druidry

References

Ahmed, A. (1999). Islam today. London. I.B. Tauris Publishers.

American Counseling Association (1995). American Counseling Association, Alexandra, VA: Author.

American Religious Identification Survey (2002). The Graduate Center of the City University of New York, 2002-NOV-22.

Association for Spiritual, Ethical and Relgious Values in Counseling (2003). American Counseling Association, Alexandra, VA: Author.

Archuletta, L. Pascua Yaqui Medicine Man. Lecture on Indigenous Medicine. Tucson, AZ: September, 12, 2001.

Assemblies of God (2003). General Council of the Assemblies of God. Retrieved 1/30/03. www.ag.org.

Baha'i World (2002). Baha'i International Community. Retrieved 2/10/03. www.bahai.org.

Baetz, M., Larson, D.B., Marcoux, G., Bowen, R., & Griffin, R. (2002). Canadian Psychiatric Inpatient Religious Commitment: An Association with Mental Health. Canadian Journal of Psychiatry. Vol. 47, Issue 2.

Beck, A. (1979). Cognitive therapy and emotional disorders. New York: Penguin Books

Beck, V. & Walters, A.L. (1977). The sacred ways of knowledge: Sources of life. Tsaile, AZ: Navajo Community College.

Bedell, K.B. (1997). Yearbook of American and Canadian Churches. Nashville, TN: Abingdon Press.

Bergin, A. & Richards, P.S. (2000). <u>Handbook of psychotherapy and religious diversity</u>. Washington DC: American Psychological Association

Beversluis, J. (Ed.) (1995) <u>A source book for earth's community of religions</u>. Grand Rapids, MI: CoNexus Press.

Bishop, D.R. (1992). Religious values in cross-cultural counseling. <u>Counseling and Values</u>, 36, 179-181.

Boadella, D. (1989). Essence and ground: Towards the understanding of spirituality in psychotherapy. <u>International Journal of Psychotherapy</u>. Vol. 3, Issue 1. Retrieved 04/27/03.

Boyd-Franklin, N. (1989). <u>Black families in therapy: a multi-systems approach</u>. New York: Guilford Press.

Campbell, D.T. (1975). On the conflicts between biological and social evolution and between psychology and moral tradition. <u>American Psychologist</u>, 30, 1103-1124.

Canda, E.R. & Furman, L.D. (1999). <u>Spiritual diversity in social work practice. The heart of helping</u>. New York: Simon and Schuster.

Christensen, C.P. (1989). Cross-cultural awareness development: A conceptual mode. <u>Counselor Educator and Supervision</u>. 28, 270-289.

Clinebell, H. (1995). <u>Counseling for spiritually empowered wholeness: A hope-centered approach</u>. New York: Hawath Pastoral Press.

Comas- Diaz, L. (1989). <u>Culturally relevant issues and treatment implications for Hispanics</u>. In D.R. Koslow & E. Salett

(Eds.) Crossing cultures in mental health. Washington,
DC: Society for International Education Training and
Research.

Corey, G. (2001). Theory and practice of counseling and
psychotherapy. Belmont, CA: Wadsworth

Cunningham, S. (1994). Wicca – A guide for the solitary
practioner. St. Paul, MN: Llewellyn Publications.
- (1997). Living Wicca. St. Paul, MN: Llewellyn
Publications

Curott, P. (1995). Wicca and nature spirituality – A portrait of
wicca. In J. Beversluis (Ed.) (1995). A source book for
earth's community of religions: New York: CoNexus
Press.

Das, A. & Kemp, S. (1997). Between two worlds: Counseling
South Asian Americans. Journal of Multicultural
Counseling and Development. 25, 23. Retrieved 09/24/01

Dass, R. & Gorman, P. (1985). How can I help? Stories and
reflections on service. New York: Knopf.

deSilva, P. (1993). Buddhism and Counseling. British Journal of
Guidance and Counseling. 21, p30-35. Retrieved 09/24/01

Drury, N. (1996). Elements of shamanism. Rockport, MA:
Element Books.

Eck, D. (2001). A new religious America. San Francisco:
HarperCollins.

Edwards, L. (2001). A brief guide to beliefs ideas, theologies,
mysteries, and movements. London: Westminster John
Knox Press.

Ehrlich, E., Flexner, S., Carruth, G., Hawkins, J. ((1986). <u>Oxford American dictionary</u>. New York: Avon Publications.

Eliade, M. (1959). <u>The sacred and the profane</u> (W.R. Trask, Trans.) New York: Harcourt Brace Jovanovich.

Ellenberger, H. (1970a). <u>The discovery of the unconscious</u>. New York: Basic Books.

The First Church of Christ, Scientist (2003). Church of Christ Scientist. Retrieved 1/30/03. <u>www.tfccs.com</u>

Fortunato, J.E. (1982). <u>Embracing the exile: Healing journeys of gay Christians</u>. New York: Harper and Row.

Foskett, J. (2001). Soul space: The pastoral care of people with major mental health problems. <u>International Review of Psychiatry</u>, Vol. 13, Issue 2.

Frankel, V. (1984). <u>Man's search for meaning</u>. London: Ruetledge.

Freud, S. (1927). <u>Future of illusion</u>. London: Hogarth Press.

(1930). <u>Civilization and its discontents</u>. London: Hogarth Press.

Fukuyama, M.A. (1990). Taking a universal approach to multicultural counseling. <u>Counselor Education and Supervision</u>, 30, 6-17.

Fukuyama, M.A. & Sevig, T.D. (1999) <u>Integrating spirituality into multicultural counseling</u>. Thousand Oaks, CA: Sage

(1997). Spiritual issues in counseling: A new course. <u>Counselor Education and Supervision</u>, 36, 233-244.

Garcia-Preto, N. (1996). Puerto Rican families. In M. McGoldrick, J. Giordano & J.K. Pearce (Eds.), Ethnicity and family therapy 2nd ed. New York: Guilford Press.

Garrett, M. (1994). The path of good medicine: Understanding and counseling Native Americans. <u>Journal of Multicultural Counseling and Development</u>. 22, p. 134. Retrieved 09/24/01

Garrett, M & Carroll, J. (2000). Mending the broken circle: Treatment of substance dependence among Native American. <u>Journal of Counseling & Development</u>, 78, p. 10. Retrieved 09/24/01

Georgia, R.T. (1994). Preparing to counsel clients of different religious background: A phenomenological approach. <u>Counseling and Values</u>. Vol. 38, Issue 2.

Guiley, R. (1999). <u>Encyclopedia of witches and witchcraft</u> 2nd Ed.New York: Facts on File, Inc.

Harner, M. (1980). <u>The way of the shaman</u>. New York: Bantam Books.

Helminiak, D.A. (1996). <u>The human core of spirituality: Mind as psyche and spirit</u>. Albany, New York: State University of New York Press

Holy Bible (1984). Grand Rapids, MI: Zondervan Publishing House.

Iyer, R. (1994). <u>The essentail writings of Mahatma Gandhi</u>. Oxford: Oxford University Press.

James, W. (1982). <u>The varieties of religious experience</u>. Liguori, MO. Triumph Books.

Johnson, W.B. & Ridley, C.R. (1992). Brief Christian and non-Christian rational-emotive therapy with depressed Christian clients. <u>Counseling and Values</u>. 36, 220-229.

Jung, C. (1938). <u>Psychology and religion</u>. New Haven, CT: Yale
University Press.

Kernberg, O. (1996). <u>Psychoanalysis and religion</u>. Speech at the
1st World Congress of Psychotherapy, Vienna, July.

Kulwicki, A. (1999). <u>Health issues among Arab Muslim families</u>.
In B. Aswad & B. Bilge (Eds.) Family and gender among
American Muslims. Philadelphia, PA: Temple Press.

Libreria Editrice Vaticana ((1994). <u>Catechism of the Catholic
Church</u>. Liguori, MO: Liguori Publications.

Lomawaima, H. Hopi Elder. Lecture on the Hopi People.
Tucson, AZ. August, 28, 2001.

Magida, A. (Ed.) (1996). <u>How to be a perfect stranger</u>.
Woodstock, VT: Jewish Lights Publishing.

Matthews, J. (Ed.) (1999). <u>The druid source book</u>. New York:
Sterling Publishing

Matthews, D. & Clark, C. (1998). <u>The faith factor. Proof of
healing power of prayer</u>. New York: Penguin Books.

Mbiti, J.S. (1991). <u>Introduction to African religion</u> 2nd ed.
Oxford, England: Heinemann Educational Publishers.
- (1970). <u>African religions and philosophy</u>. London:
Heinemann Educational Publishers.

Nobles, W. (1980). <u>African philosophy: Foundations for black
psychology</u>. In R. Jones (Ed.) Black Psychology 2nd. ed.
New York: Harper & Row.

- (1972). <u>African philosophy Foundations for black psychology</u>.
In R. Jones (Ed.) Black Psychology 1st ed. New York:
Harper & Row.

Office of Public Information of Jehovah's Witnesses. (2003). Watch Tower Bible and Tract society of Pennsylvania. Retrieved 2/10/03. www.jw-media.org.

Paniagua, F. (1998). <u>Assessing and treating culturally diverse clients</u> 2nd ed. Thousand Oaks, CA: Sage Publications.

Parziale, J. (2003). <u>Perspectives on Presbyterian religions review</u>. Tucson, AZ.

Population Reference Bureau (2003). PRB. Online. Retrieved 2/10/03. www.prb.org.

Prager, D. & Telushkin J. (1986). <u>The nine questions people ask about Judaism</u>. New York: Simon & Schuster.

Princeton Religion Research of Center. <u>Religion in America</u>. Gallup Poll. 1996: Princeton, N.J.

Price, J.A. (1975). <u>An applied analysis of North American Indian drinking patterns</u>. Human Organization, 34, 17-26.

Ramisetty-Milker, S. (1993). Asian Indian Immigrants in America and Socio-cultural Issues in Counseling. <u>Journal of Multicultural Counseling & Development</u>, 21,p.36. Retrieved 09/24/01.

Religious Movements (2003). Retrieved 1/30/03. Religiousmovements.lib.virginia.edu.

Renard, J. (2002). <u>The handy religion answer book</u>. Canton, MI: Visible Ink Press.

Renouf, J. (2003). <u>Perspectives on world religions review</u>. Tucson, AZ

Richards, P.S., Rector, J., & Tjeltveit, A. (2000). From integrating spirituality into treatment. <u>Values, Spirituality and Psychotherapy</u>. Washington, D.C: American Psychological Association.

Robbins, S.P., Canada, E.R. & Chatterjee, P. (1998). <u>Contemporary human behavior theory: A critical perspective for social work.</u> Boston: Allyn & Bacon.

Roots, K. (2003). New index tracks spiritual state of nation. <u>Research News Opportunity in Science and Theology</u>. Vol. 3, No. 9.

Rosten, L. (Ed.) (1975) <u>Religions of America</u>. New York: Simon & Schuster

Rubin, J.B. (1996). <u>Psychotherapy and Buddhism: Toward an integration</u>. New York: Plenum.

Saur, M. & Saur, W. (1990). <u>Spiritual themes and religious responses test</u>. Unpublished manuscript.

Scorzelli, J. & Reinke-Scorzelli, M. (2001). Cultural sensitivity and cognitive therapy in Thailand. <u>Journal of Mental Health and Counseling</u>, 23, 85-88. Retrieved 09/24/01

Shafranske, E.P. (Ed.)(1996). <u>Religion and the clinical practice of psychology</u>. Washington, DC: American Psychological Association.

Shafranske, E.P. & Maloney, H.N. (1990). <u>Religion and the clinical practice of psychology: A case for inclusion</u>. In E.P. Shafranske (Ed.) Religion and the clinical practice of psychology. Washington, DC: American Psychological Association.

Sloat, D. (1990). <u>Growing up holy and wholly: Understanding and hope for adult children of Evangelicals.</u> Brentwood, NJ: Wolgemugh & Hyatt.

Smith, H. (1991) <u>The Religions of man</u>. New York: New American Library.

Smith, W.C. (1985). <u>The church in the life of the black family</u>. Valley Forge, PA: Judson Press.

Sue, D.W. (1992). The challenge of multiculturalism: The road less traveled. <u>American Counselor</u>, 1 (1), 6-14.

Sue, D. & Sue, D. (2003). <u>Counseling the culturally diverse</u> 4th Ed. New York: John Wiley & Sons.

Sue, S., Allen, D.B. & Conaway, L. (1981). The responsiveness and equality of mental health care to Chicanos and Native Americans. <u>American Journal of Community Psychology</u>, 6, 137-146.

Tseng, W.S. & McDermott, J.F. (1981). <u>Culture, mind and therapy: An introduction to cultural psychiatry.</u> New York: Brunner/Mazel.

U.S. Bureau of the Census (1991). <u>Census of population: Social and economy characteristics, American Indian and Alaska Native areas.</u> Washington DC: U.S. Government Printing Office

U.S. Department of Health and Human Services. (1990). A National Health Plan for Native American Mental Health Services (amended 1995). Washington DC: Author

Van Kaam, A. (1983-1995). <u>Formative spirituality</u>. Vol. 1-7. New York: Crossroads.

Walsh, F. (Ed.) (1999). <u>Spiritual resources in family therapy</u>. New York: Guilford Press.

Wilber, K. (1995). <u>Sex, ecology, and spirit</u>. Boston: Shambalah.

Wink, W. (1998). The powers that Be. Theology for a new millennium. New York: Double Day.

Wormser, R. (1994). American Islam: Growing up Muslim in America. New York: Walker Publishing.

Worthington, E.L. (1989). Religious faith across the life span. Implications for counseling and research. The Counseling Psychologist. 17, 555-612.

Wright, J.W. (1994). Universal almanac. New York: Andrews & McMeel.

Wulf, D.M. (1991). Psychology of religion: Classic and contemporary view. New York: Wiley.

Yamamoto, J. (1986). Therapy for Asian Americans and Pacific Islanders. In C.B. Wilkinson (Ed.) Ethnic psychiatry. New York: Plenum.

Yao, R. (1987, August - September). Addiction and the fundamental experience. Paper presented at the 95th annual convention of the American Psychological Association. New York, NY.

Yearbook of American & Canadian Churches, 70th ed. (2002). National Council of Churches. New York: National Council of the Churches of Christ in the USA.

Zepeda, Fernando (2005). Editing support and recommendation: La Frontera Inc. Tucson, AZ.

About the Author

Reverend Janine d'Haven has focused her ministry and her psychotherapy practice on a diverse population for several years serving and honoring multicultural clients. She is an Interfaith Minister who studied all faith traditions as if they were her own. Reverend d'Haven holds Master Degrees in both Counseling and Psychology and Divinity. She is also an Interfaith Spiritual Director. In addition, she teaches multicultural competencies from a religious and spiritual perspective to helping professionals. She is an advisor for graduate and undergraduate students at a private college in the Southwest.

35669605R00093

Made in the USA
San Bernardino, CA
13 May 2019